KU-266-996

(Ste)

WITHDRAWN
Developing the
Global Teacher

Developing the Global Teacher

Theory and Practice in Initial Teacher Education

Edited by Miriam Steiner

Trentham Books

in association with World Studies Trust

First published in 1996 by
Trentham Books Limited

Trentham Books Limited
Westview House
734 London Road
Oakhill
Stoke-on-Trent
Staffordshire
England ST4 5NP

British Cataloguing in Publication Data
A catalogue record for this book is available
from the British Library
ISBN 1 85856 032 2

Designed and typeset by Trentham Print Design
Ltd., Chester and printed in Great Britain by
Bemrose Shafron (Printers) Limited, Chester.

Contents

Section II: Pedagogies, Partnerships and Practices

Foreword

Professor Tim Brighouse

The world shrinks as the telecommunications revolution accelerates. If we are educated and rich we can belong to many communities, while the poorer and more ignorant we are, the more we are restricted to the community of place.

The urgency of the issue of global education is obvious if you work and live as I do in Birmingham, a city of a thousand trades and a hundred ethnic communities where the diversity of the many strongly held faiths, on the one hand, and faithlessness, on the other, add to the potential wealth and the present challenge of those who would educate tomorrow's citizens. We struggle to see bilingualism not as a problem but as a rich opportunity to create a city in the United Kingdom that is truly multilingual. Whether one lives in Birmingham or not, the reality for those who teach in Britain today is that they must think globally while teaching locally.

George Walker, in the Harry Ree memorial lecture this spring, put the issues vividly. 'Why', he asked, should students worry about the 90 million annual increase in the world's population ... the 400 million unemployed in the 'South', the annual global per capita expenditure on the UN of $1.90 compared to an arms expenditure of $150, ozone depletion, drought, famine and poverty?

There is of course one very obvious reason. Anyone ... over the age of 50, given reasonably good luck, can expect life to go on much as it is now until we achieve our generous life expectancy. Those of you between 20 and 50 will need unusually good luck for that to happen and anyone under 20 ... has no chance at all. Something is going to have to change and this creates what a distinguished US ambassador to the UN ... recently described as 'the culture of necessity'.

But if the issue is pressing, it is no less formidable a challenge. It is difficult enough, for example, to tackle equal opportunity within the artificial framework of the particular nation or local community within which we teach — and very few schools have made much of a fist of it across the full range of issues affecting gender, race, religion and social class. It is breathtaking, however, to try to take on the global issues so starkly set out by George Walker and the other enthusiasts who variously push development or global education as part of their pedagogical credo. Yet that is what this book seeks to do. It does so nobly across a range of issues and touching a whole range of possible entry points for the reader — whose work and interests lie in primary, secondary, special or further and higher education.

A starting point for action — whether one is in a school, college, or university and whether as governor, lecturer, teacher, (including student or newly qualified), support staff or whatever — ought to be a set of principles.

I should like to stake out a claim for five principles which should govern those of us who try to encourage the global approach to education — which applies to everyone concerned with the task of educating the next generation. I set them out as point and counterpoint in order to sharpen the focus of the principle, or assumption, or proposition being advanced.

Schooling and education should be based on the goal of everyone achieving success rather than allowing success for some and failure for others

Most schooling systems have been based on the assumption that success cannot be rationed and that there must be failure for some or many. As long ago as 1804 the Bishop of London stated that:

> Men (sic) of considerable ability say that it is safest for the church and the state that the lower classes should remain in that state of ignorance in which nature has originally placed them.

Just before the 1870 Education Act, Robert Lowe, the architect of the Revised Code (which was the instrument of measuring the efficacy of the first attempt at universal education), reminded providers that:

> The education of the lower classes should be just sufficient to give them that sense of awe for higher education which the leaders of the nation demand.

In modern schools the consciousness of league tables leads to attention to some at the expense of others — for example, attention to the proportion of those obtaining or likely to obtain five or more higher grades in GCSE at the expense of the many who will not. Differential value is implied by the institutional practices of schools — awards evenings, rewards, assemblies, for example.

Places of education espousing success for everyone will always be seeking new ways to unlock and to celebrate both the release and flourishing of potential and will also collect evidence and monitor outcomes in general and particularly seek to ascertain how closely they were achieving their bold ambition. Schools with these goals would be able to tell you the comparative overall performance of black, mixed race, the different Asian groups and white children and, in each case, between boys and girls. They will have in place practices which soften the effect of poverty and remove the barriers of disadvantage. Typically such schools would see bullying, racism, violence and harassment as the unwelcome fellow travellers of any community, including their own. Institutions at all levels would have established practices and monitoring arrangements which would enable them continuously to improve.

Schooling and education should be based on the assumption that intelligence is multi-faceted not general, environmentally affected as well as inherited, and limitless not fixed

The work of Howard Gardner (1) illustrates the best known and most important example of that assumption. Gardner argues that there are seven sorts of intelligence — literate; numerate/logical/scientific; musical; spatial; motor; intrapersonal and interpersonal.

The implications for schools and teaching are enormous. It would be beholden on a school committed to Gardner's assumption that all schemes of work would be designed to appeal to each of the seven intelligences. Teaching would be so arranged to cover preferably all, but at least four or five, of the intelligences, to give pupils an optimum chance of understanding and of stretching towards their potential. 'Mixed-ability' classes become a conun- drum to define under such a view of intelligence. There are powerful implications for the rewards and celebratory system of the school and for the local education authority there are some uncomfortable imperatives to overhaul their awards systems.

Schooling and education should be based on the assumption that learning is a lifelong not a 'once and for all' activity

Most phases of schooling provision are insulated one from the other. Discontinuity is seen as a chronic problem. Too many teachers and support staff fail to realise the crucial importance of providing a personal example to their pupils of being a lifelong learner. To be seen to be taking pleasure in reading; being in the library/resource centre using books, materials and IT; mixing staff in-service work with pupils; inviting back old pupils; filling the walls of school halls with the many-sided activities of former members of the school community; using awards evenings to celebrate the learning success of the whole community, not merely the pupils; arranging opportunities for pupils from your own school to tutor and learn with children from another phase of education in 'tutoring' schemes — all are practical expressions of the lifelong learning community.

Schooling and education should be based on the assumption that competition is best when ipsatively rather than normatively based

By 'ipsative' I mean based on competition against 'oneself' rather than others. The best teachers are always seeking to find ways of surprising their students into doing or understanding something they did not think they could do before. The worst are too idle to understand individual difference, and fall back on the crutch of 'form orders' which compare child with child. That is not to say there is no place for the latter, but it needs to be used sparingly and often for the group rather than for an individual. This over-reliance on the normative is the great failure of Ofsted and the league table approach to school performance. 'Improving against previous personal best' is not a bad taskmaster for the learner. This is true at any age. When young it provides the spur and by the time you are old you perhaps have the wisdom and contentment to relax slightly in the knowledge of being past personal best.

Schooling and education should be based on the assumption of inclusive not exclusive practices

In a sense this assumption is the most important of all. It implies that we are all different but equal and that our society should be striving to accommodate difference within a community seeking the highest common factor of shared values. Inclusive education is subtly different from integrated provision. For me a truly inclusive school would never permanently exclude a child even if for long periods it had to arrange for the child to receive education elsewhere.

It seems to me that these five principles or assumptions are mutually reinforcing. We have a long way to go to boast schools or education systems which live the reality of these five principles but in a global context they are essential.

What I personally find baffling — a problem to which I cannot imagine a solution — is how one translates such values from an insular single nation perspective into a universal global context. Thus, I return to my quotations from George Walker.

We might console ourselves with the thought that if progress is possible locally in matters within our grasp, then the next generation will find some of the solutions. To do so they will need to ask the right questions. And in that respect this book will be invaluable.

Notes

1. See, most recently, Gardner, H. (1991) *The Unschooled Mind*, London: Fontana.

Initial Teacher Education and Global Citizenship: An Introduction

Miriam Steiner

Citizenship and community are the catch phrases of the nineteen-nineties as we search for solutions to current social dilemmas on both the national and international stages. That they are necessary and that a global society is in the process of being formed is beyond question. Addressing the meanings and implications of global citizenship now, in this period of flux, seems not visionary but sensible and prudent. The authors of this book would agree with Lynch's paradigm for citizenship education:

> For educators the challenge of the 1990s is to deliver not just education for citizenship of a pluralist democracy, but education for active global democracy, founded on universal values about the nature of human beings and their social behaviour ... (this education should be set in) a global context of human rights and social responsibilities, contributing to the achievement of democratic values and behaviour in pluralistic societies and in a culturally diverse world... Schools have a unique and indispensable function in the legitimation of justice within global pluralism and sustainable development ... (Lynch, 1992)

A broad outlook, wider set of loyalties and commitment to justice at local, national and international levels have always been at the heart of global education. Certain terms recur — *development education, global education, education for sustainable development, environmental education, education for the future, world studies, education for international understanding.* Just as education for race equality and education for gender equality lose their singularity if always subsumed under the common title of 'education for equal opportunities', so here too it's important to preserve distinctiveness. You will find that the writers in this book have tended to use 'world studies' and 'global education' interchangeably.

The chapter by Robin Richardson describes the history and development of this domain. It also provides us with a concise analytical framework which clearly and powerfully demonstrates how citizenship is an ideal concept to define our social identities and rights and obligations, both national and global.

Antecedents: 'Third World perspectives in initial teacher training'

The authors here are writing about their recent experiences of ITE which has continued the global approach to work which has been going on steadily throughout the country over many years, sometimes in a climate positively disposed to its values, more usually not.

Twenty years ago, Oxfam's Education Department set up a project in two Colleges of Education to introduce 'Third World' perspectives (entitled 'Third World Perspectives in Initial Teacher Training'). The underlying premise was that '..acquaintance with the 'Third World' could help a teacher become a better teacher, no matter what his or her special subject was' (Thomas, 1979).

This necessary knowledge didn't only entail information about 'developing countries', but should also be about '...some of the most original and interesting philosophies of education developed in the 20th century ... (which) have originated in the 'Third World' ... (those of Tagore, Gandhi, Vinoba, Julius Nyerere, Paolo Freire and Ivan Illich.' (ibid). It would

be interesting to discover how many School of Education libraries stock these works even now!

Two courses are described in Thomas's project report; both were innovative in their methodologies and contents and made a significant contribution to the then relatively new fields of world studies and development education. Describing his project at that time, Robin Richardson summarised what seemed to him the 'main agenda' of the student teachers in his group:

> How to view the education which one has oneself received, and is receiving, and about to pass on to others? How to resist, and how to avoid engaging in, indoctrination? How to speak up for oneself, and take a hand in shaping the conditions of one's life? How to approach other cultures? How to help other human beings to learn? How to become a woman in modern society? How to view one's own immediate future as, very probably, an unemployed teacher? (ibid)

These questions seem as pertinent today.

The background to this book

The following chapters are the outcome of a contemporary project set up with similar goals and values to the one of 1976. The book is the product of a collaborative project between ITE tutors at twelve University Schools of Education and education workers from a range of local and national non-governmental organisations (NGOs) promoting world studies, development and global education. The agencies involved were ActionAid, CAFOD, Christian Aid, Oxfam, Save the

Children and UNICEF; the NGOs included the World Studies Project, Manchester; Centre for Global Education, York; Global Futures Project, Bath; Lancashire Development Education Group, Preston; Southern Voices, Manchester; World Education Project, Bangor. The higher education institutions (HEIs) are those of the book's authors as well as colleagues at the University of Derby and St Martin's College, Lancaster.

Our common goal was to share experiences and insights and develop approaches (courses and modules) which would enable new teachers to bring a global perspective into the curriculum and teach in ways that foster democratic values and skills. Our partnership started in the first term of 1993 and thus has coincided with one of the most intense periods of upheaval in ITE in memory. During this time we've seen the emergence of the 'new' universities, the establishment of the Teacher Training Agency (TTA), a change in accreditation procedures, the proclamation of a set of professional competences for qualifying teachers (Department for Education (DfE) 14/93), new course structures, evolving relationships with schools, new Ofsted criteria and, of course, the revision of the National Curriculum, following the Dearing consultation.

These government-imposed 'reforms' will have serious long-term consequences for education, not only because they will alter the length and content of teacher education courses but also because the technocratic values promoted by documents such as DfE 14/93 undermine the craft of education. This specifies the professional competences for newly qualifying teachers which most HEIs have now adapted and expanded. New teachers are to be 'trained' in the techniques of classroom management rather than 'educated' in the holistic processes of teaching. Writers throughout this book refer to this document and, in Chapter 5, Nick Clough and Cathie Holden propose a supplementary list of competences aimed at developing a more rounded 'global teacher'. The current trend, in which the processes of education are reduced, at all levels, to blocks of testable outcomes, seems more to threaten the development of democratic skills than to enhance democratic citizenship.

The contributors to this book are concerned also to look beyond the goal of creating a more democratic, humane and just society in Britain. We believe that citizenship needs to be conceived of as more than loyalty to one's country of birth and respect for its laws; it's about membership of the global community and an active commitment to advancing universal human rights, material and environmental welfare, peace and democracy for everyone.

Global Citizenship perspectives in initial teacher education

What about the other starting point of the 1976 project? Is it still important for student teachers to know about the 'Third World'?

It could be argued that this generation knows more about it than ever before. 'Band Aid' and 'Live Aid' have made images of despair and of positive development commonplace. 'Interdependence' is no longer the catch phrase of only the development lobby, but a profoundly accurate description of the global condition: economic, cultural, environmental and social. The world's peoples all shop in the global shopping mall, not only in the affluent North, but also in rural markets world-wide where goods from Eastern Europe and China abound. Consumers of entertainment and information on every continent make their choices in the cultural bazaar as Princess Di, CNN and 'Dallas' are beamed to remote villages whose artefacts and crafts are in turn an everyday part of the North's decor and cuisine. Globally dispersed production lines and finance markets never close as the 'virtual economy' is linked around the clock by satellite and computer.

It is a world dominated by supranational production and trading forces, international cultural icons and common environmental problems on the one hand, and intensified and often painful expressions of local identity and regional singularity on the other. The conservative hegemony of the past fifteen years seems to have made it unfashionable to be committed to projects of social and economic improvement. But the realities of unequal trade and debt have not changed; nor has the arms trade or the unnecessary deaths of children from hunger. Are student teachers being equipped to deal themselves, and to prepare their pupils to deal, with these painful realities and with accelerating processes of change?

Our partnership covered more ground than the Oxfam/ITE one of 1976. Both ITE and the NGOs have expanded and become more intensely professionalised since 1976. There are now many more national and local development education agencies and centres producing a wide range of educational materials which provide pertinent information about Southern situations and places, and model the best classroom practice. These developments are explored in Marjorie Drake's chapter. In fact the student-centred methodologies of educators like Freire and the others in Thomas's list have become internationally widespread (eg Apple, 1993 and hooks, 1994, both discuss their debt to Freire; also Osler, 1994). We are also more able to meet face to face with students and teachers from the South studying or working here and Jaya Graves' chapter provides both a compelling rationale and useful guidelines for doing this.

Our goals were the same as in 1976: increased knowledge and understanding of the conditions of life in what we now call the 'South' rather than the 'Third World'; of the impact of consumer and environmental decisions on the welfare of ecological and human systems; the importance of releasing individual energy and creativity through non-authoritarian teaching. In 1976 and 1977, the Oxfam project participants were able to design specific courses to do this and until recently many HEIs offered 'options' on PGCE and undergraduate courses with similar aims. The case studies from Wales and Ireland in this book provide exemplars of such tailor-made courses (Bennell *et al* and Brennan). But the pressures of the National Curriculum and the 're-forming' (and 'de-forming') of ITE mean that, on the whole, even these marginalised courses are no longer available. That they were optional in the first place was shocking, since learning how to integrate moral and social issues that have both local and global implications ought to be an entitlement in all ITE courses.

The change in title from 'Third World' to 'Global Citizenship' also represents a shift in consciousness since the first project. Pictures from space have helped humanity visualise its connectedness and phrases such as 'Spaceship Earth' have entered the collective consciousness. The apparent dissolution of ideological and geographical power blocs and the growth of transnational economic trading communities have created a sense that frontiers and borders are of less importance and significance. Shifting patterns of nationality and nationalism have also focused our attention on the meaning of the state and the citizen. If, as Dahrendorff predicted in 1990, we are in the midst of the decade of citizenship, we ought to be forging meanings for this concept which can serve us better in the future when, we hope, the current regional restructurings and upheavals have subsided (Dahrendorff, 1990).

Citizenship has also been on the official agenda for education in the UK in this decade. *Education for Citizenship* was designated one of five non-statutory, cross-curricular themes that were intended to permeate the curriculum (NCC, 1990). The official guidance document presented an ostensibly unproblematic account of 'the knowledge, skills, and attitudes necessary for exploring, making informed decisions about and exercising responsibilities and rights in

a democratic society' (ibid). The context was distinctly national with the occasional reference to Europe and the rest of the world ('Individuals have obligations to and relationships with national, European and world-wide communities' (ibid).

Yet despite also being the subject of a separate Commission set up by the Speaker of the House of Commons, citizenship education seems to have had little impact in schools or ITE courses. In September 1995, Nick Tate, the chief executive of the School Curriculum and Assessment Authority, reported that 87 percent of primary and 80 percent of secondary schools recently surveyed had rated citizenship work 'not essential' (Tate,1995). Tate, himself criticised for an earlier article that offered a limited, anglo-centric view of 'Britishness' (see, inter alia, Richardson, 1995), suggests that citizenship education is not taken seriously in England and Wales because 'We have always seen ourselves as 'subjects'. He goes on to urge the necessity of citizenship education in the face of what he fears is a breakdown in community spirit and in the processes of transmitting national values of 'honesty, self-denial, loyalty, responsibility and a respect for truth' (op. cit.).

Is he right about the British seeing themselves as 'subjects'? Are the values he cites enough to build a sense of community — whether local, national or global?

Research I have recently conducted with undergraduate student teachers would seem to contradict his assertion. A 'subject' is, *inter alia*, 'subordinate, subservient, dependent, ... a thing over which a legal right is exercised' as well as being 'one who owes allegiance to a sovereign, a state...' (Kirkpatrick, 1983). When we asked small groups of student teachers (99 individuals) to complete the open-ended question '*To me being a citizen means...*', the key issues that emerged were: *Community* (belonging and contributing to, taking responsibility for others); *Rights* (protecting one's own and advancing others'); *Identity* (national and personal, (often expressed as feeling free to be an individual)) and the *global dimension*. This latter was expressed by sentiments such as, '... being a member of a community not confined by culture, language and boundaries'; 'I am part of society and mankind (sic)' (Steiner and Voiels, 1995).

Their replies were pervaded by an undercurrent of 'the people versus government', suggesting that, if they saw themselves as 'subjects', it was as subjects wary and suspicious of the state. In fact, membership of the European community was seen as a means of protecting and increasing their civil rights. Whether asked to define citizenship in general or European citizenship in particular, notions of national pride were not very significant. They were clearly relaxed about constructing their identities as British, European and global citizens and didn't show any signs of the 'crisis of identity' often feared by the right. They seemed comfortable with diversity and were not '..bewildered, schizophrenic, unhappy and lonely' (Roberts, 1995).

It is interesting to note, as I discuss below in chapter 3, that these student teachers had little experience in their schooling of handling political concepts such as democracy, human rights or social justice; in no sense could they be said to have had much education either about or for citizenship. Yet their attitudes do not, in my opinion, bode ill for the condition of citizenship. There was a clear sense in our discussions that they think citizenship is something wider than loyalty to one's community of birth (or adoption) and its laws. A significant number sited their commitment to 'community' and concern for the environment and human rights in a global context.

Concepts for global citizenship

Recent writers on global citizenship (eg Heater, 1990; Lynch, 1992; Falk, 1994; van Steenbergen, 1994; Huckle, 1996) point to the complexity of this concept. Marshall's categorisation of citizenship as concerning the *civil, political* and *social* is no longer adequate in the context where supranational economic forces and common environmental problems know no boundaries (Marshall, 1950). The public sphere in which the citizen can exercise his or her rights has been broadened by international conventions and courts of law. Van Steenbergen suggests that new types of citizenship '..are unfolded in the light of new developments and problems with which we are confronted today: cultural citizenship, active citizenship, race-neutral and gender-neutral citizenship, European citizenship, global citizenship and ecological citizenship' (op cit).

Looking at *global* citizenship specifically, both Lynch (1992) and Falk (1994) clearly identify the visionary component that often informs thinking about the topic.

... the extension of citizenship to its global domain tends to be aspirational in spirit, drawing on a long tradition of thought and feeling about the ultimate unity of human experience, giving rise to a politics of desire that posits for the planet as a whole a set of conditions of peace and justice and sustainability (Falk, 1994).

We see this in action in a range of grassroots concerns — from human rights and environmental activism to international 'solidarity' movements supporting local freedom campaigns or national liberation struggles. Falk also describes other versions of the 'global citizen' now emerging: global businesspersons whose travelling experiences and attachment to the over-riding dictates of commerce may lead them to lose '...any sense of cultural specificity that could be connected with a specific attachment with place or community' (ibid:134); the functional would-be managers of the 'global order' — whether economic, environmental or military, acting without vision to maintain the *status quo* of Northern life-styles.

The themes of international understanding, justice and human rights, sustainable development and cultural pluralism are woven through the practical and analytical chapters which follow,written by ITE tutors and by education professionals from NGOs. John Huckle explains why student teachers need to be aware of some of the recent trends in social and political thought which underpin growing globalisation. The domain of Futures Education is represented by David Hicks and Kay Woods who describe an innovative new course. Sue Lyle's work with B.Ed. students at Swansea shows how Environmental Education for Sustainable Futures can be a central aspect of a traditional course. The implications for institutional arrangements are explored by Gillian Klein and Sneh Shah, while others offer practical examples of innovative teaching and research in a range of traditional disciplines (Margot and Kim Brown, Heather Norris Nicolson, Chris Rowley and Nigel Toye, Julia Tanner and Veronica Voiels). I look at more general aspects of what it means to be a global teacher within the current debates about the social functions of education.

Pervading all the pragmatic or idealistic articulations of global citizenship described in this introduction is the sense that their realisation in one form or another is only a matter of time. The authors of this book would urge that the project of redefining and refining communitarian values and sharpening commitment to universal welfare are necessary *now* so that a 'global citizen' will mean someone who actually experiences unquestioned human rights and a more just distribution of global resources rather than it becoming a new term for the old unequal realities.

Contributors

Bath College of Higher Education: David Hicks and Kay Wood

Charlotte Mason College, University of Lancaster: Chris Rowley and Nigel Toye

Coleg Normal, Bangor: Cynrig Hughes

De Montfort University, Bedford: John Huckle

Leeds Metropolitan University: Julia Tanner

Manchester Metropolitan University: Miriam Steiner and Veronica Voiels

Swansea Institute: Sue Lyle

University College of Ripon and York St John: Heather Norris Nicholson

University of Exeter: Cathie Holden

University of Hertfordshire: Sneh Shah

University of the West of England: Nick Clough

University of Warwick: Gillian Klein

Centre for Global Education, University College of Ripon and York St John: Margot Brown and Kim Brown

Development Education Support Centre, Dublin: Fionnuala Brennan

Global Futures Project, Bath College of Higher Education: David Hicks

Lancashire Development Education Group: Marjorie Drake

Môn and Arfon Central America Group: Patricia Daniel

Southern Voices, Manchester: Jaya Graves

World Education Project, University of Wales, Bangor: Sheila Bennell

World Studies Project, Manchester Metropolitan University: Miriam Steiner

Professor Tim Brighouse is Chief Education Officer for Birmingham

Robin Richardson is the Director of the Runnymede Trust

SECTION I
Principles and Contexts for Developing the Global Teacher

CHAPTER 1

The Terrestrial Teacher

Robin Richardson

Introduction

In order to begin preparing this chapter I took down various books from my shelves and leafed through them. As I did so, a printed card fell from one of them to the floor. I picked it up and read it. Memories seeped, then flooded, into my mind: memories of one person, and of his life's work. A brief account of these memories will help to introduce the historical background of this whole book, and will set the scene for some reflections on two of the book's principal recurring themes, to do with citizenship in general and world or global citizenship in particular.

'You are invited,' said the card, 'to a celebration of the life of James Lewis Henderson, 4 July 1910-19 April 1986.' I recalled that evening in midsummer 1986, the conversations with Jim's friends and family, the great and delightful diversity amongst his former students and colleagues, the music played to us by children from the nearby Yehudi Menuhin School, the vast converted barn in a Surrey village where the occasion took place. I recalled also the day in 1972 when I first met Jim, in a dark and dusty office in

Westminster just over the road from the House of Commons. I thought of Jim the writer and lecturer, his passionate and vigorous interest in Jungian psychology as well as in world order and world politics, his explorations of the borderlands where depth psychology meets with religious faith, and his insistent and recurring emphasis on the skills and qualities of what he called 'the terrestrial teacher'.[1]

In the 1950s and 1960s Jim Henderson was the much respected mentor of countless students at the University of London Institute of Education. He worked out with them how to teach history with a world-centred, not a national or nationalistic, perspective and he sent them out, year on year and wave on wave, to embody his ideas in classrooms up and down the country. Many of them in due course became headteachers, inspectors and teacher educators and thus were able to spread his ideas even further.

My strongest and warmest memories are of Jim in the 1970s, tirelessly setting up, leading, steering and chairing a cornucopia of projects, committees, working parties, councils, conferences, events, centres, associations, units, programmes, all of them concerned in one way or another with the educational movement to which he had devoted at least thirty years of his professional life and whose name he had himself coined and nurtured: 'world studies'.[2]

The world studies movement

The world studies movement in Britain did not die out — it did not even falter — with Jim's own passing. On the contrary, as the chapters of this book vividly show, it has gone from strength to strength. Individuals who never met Jim Henderson personally, and who indeed have never even heard of him and do not know that it was he who pioneered the paths they now tread, have worked with relentless energy and commitment to promote and realise his vision of an education system which creates and develops world citizens through what might be called a world, as distinct from a national, curriculum. Not everyone working with this vision uses the actual term 'world studies' to summarise and articulate their concerns. Other key terms which have won and mobilised people's energy in this field over the years include peace education, itself based on the insights of peace research; the green movement and environmental education; anti-racist and multicultural education; the women's movement and the creation of equal opportunities for all; human rights education; futures education; and, by no means least, development education. In latter years the generic term for this overall field has been global education; this has the advantage over 'world studies' of

implying a cross-curricular theme or dimension rather than a time-tabled subject.

In practice, all these terms mingle and overlap with each other in their day-to-day meanings. In all areas of the overall field there is a concern for issues of practical classroom pedagogy, such that pupils and students in schools learn not only about the wider world ('world society', 'one world', 'spaceship earth', 'the global village', and so forth) but also, simultaneously, about themselves, their immediate and close relationships and their local neighbourhoods. The theoretical underpinning for much of this pedagogy has come from the work of Paulo Freire, and that of Freire's followers and co-workers throughout the world. The field is of fascinating and inspiring importance for all who aspire to be terrestrial teachers, and all whose task is to train and develop such teachers.

Just as world studies did not end with Jim Henderson so also it did not start with him. With every important movement in education, as in all other fields of endeavour, it is difficult or impossible to identify the starting-point with accuracy and confidence. This is certainly the case with world studies. The origins lie at least as far back as the 1880s and 1890s. At around that time there developed in many different countries a fierce critique of traditional education, built as it was on tightly drawn dichotomies between mind and body, science and art, fact and value, work and learning. Various experimental schools were set up by pioneers and idealists around the world, the most famous being Rabindranath Tagore in India. In the early years of the twentieth century these pioneers began to make increasing contact with each other across national borders and to explore commonalities. In this way they began to develop the internationalism which was already latent, but not yet much articulated, in their educational philosophy.

Transnational contacts were of course minimal in the period 1914-1918, but immediately after the war large international gatherings began to take place under the banner of 'New Education'. In due course the New Education Fellowship (NEF) was set up, with branches in many countries. Later in the century it changed its name to World Education Fellowship (WEF). Its journal *The New Era* was started in the early 1920s and is still regularly published seventy years later. Jim Henderson was much inspired by the New Education movement from about 1930 onwards and was a leading and active member of the WEF for over 50 years. A journal which he founded, the *World Studies Bulletin*, was incorporated in the 1970s into *The New Era*.

The NEF/WEF was strongly influenced in the 1930s by the League of Nations, and by the attendant belief that new educational systems and curricula were required throughout the world in order to sustain and strengthen the new world order and peace which, it was seriously believed by many at that time, were coming into being. There is a bitter irony — but also, be it noted and affirmed, a symbol of dogged hopefulness — in the fact that the organisation which most explicitly represented and articulated these ideals in Britain, the Council for Education in World Citizenship (CEWC), came into being on almost exactly the same day that the second world war broke out. CEWC, like the WEF and *The New Era*, is still going strong.

Citizenship: four components

What, though, is world citizenship? What, therefore, is education for or in world citizenship? What, for that matter, is citizenship, and education for citizenship? For a range of cultural, political and psychological reasons these questions are likely to return to centre-stage in educational debates, not only in Britain but also in most or all other countries, as the end of the present millennium approaches, and as the new millennium gets under way. This book of essays, it is reasonable to hope, will be an invaluable resource for the debates and deliberations which lie ahead, and for the embodiment and testing of the debates in practical experiment and action.

A preliminary sketch map of the field might suggest that citizenship has four main strands or dimensions. These are concerned respectively with:

☐ status, rights and obligations;

☐ social inclusion and active participation;

☐ sentiment and sense of identity; and

☐ political literacy and skill.

The first two of these are largely structural or political: amongst other things they provide and determine the context in which education for citizenship takes place. The second two are largely personal and cultural: they are more immediately relevant, therefore, to the work of teachers and teacher educators. The first and third are relatively passive and minimal: necessary components of citizenship but not sufficient. The second and fourth are relatively active and maximal: they complete the concept of citizenship and show therefore its full scope and importance. The four can be represented as a simple matrix, (see below).

The first component is to do with issues of formal status and rights, for example rights of residence, rights to take part in elections and stand for office, rights to certain welfare benefits, rights not to be discriminated against in the labour market and in access to goods and services, and so on. Also it is to do with certain minimal obligations, in particular of course the obligation to keep the law of the land. The significance of this meaning of citizenship for world studies is at present only slight. But under the Treaty of European Union there is already the possibility of people having European citizenship without being also citizens of an EU member state; and of course there is the actuality that persons with British citizenship may move freely to other EU countries and that, conversely, citizens in the rest of the EU may move freely to Britain. These rights will almost certainly, in due course, have a profound impact on conceptions of

education for citizenship. The core idea will be European citizenship not world citizenship, and there will be severe dangers in this if it is accompanied by xenophobic notions of 'Europe for the Europeans' (the term 'European' in such a phrase being code for white) but at least it will involve a move away from the narrow nationalisms and parochialisms which have pulled Europe apart in the past.

The second component is to do with social inclusion: not just the absence of discrimination but, rather, the lively presence of many opportunities and spaces for citizens and residents to take part in the cultural, economic and political affairs of the community. The term 'community' here refers to a local neighbourhood; to the internal structure of an organisation or institution; to a national state; and, in an age of increasing globalisation, to a wide range of supranational and transnational networks, relationships and collectivities. This second meaning of citizenship most certainly has many implications for world studies, for pupils and students have to develop skills in moving assertively into the transnational opportunities of the wider world, and have to appreciate and take account of the ways in which their inclusion and participation in local affairs, and in the affairs of their own nation, may influence, and may be

Tabulation: Four Compenents Of Citizenship

	Structural/Political	**Cultural/Personal**
Minimal	Rights	Identity
Maximal	Inclusion	Competence

influenced by, events and trends elsewhere.

The third component is to do with sentiments, loyalties and — as the term increasingly is — identity. Enormous amounts of energy are likely to be expended on this topic over the next few years, particularly in the context of the millennium celebrations. Who are 'we' and who are 'they', and how should we feel towards, how should we value, the self and others? Notions of cultural, ethnic and national identity exercise politicians of all parties, as they manoeuvre and bid for electoral support, and as they seek to diminish the attractions of their opponents and rivals. Also they exercise academics throughout the social sciences. And they matter profoundly to all the rest of us as well, in our daily lives and sense of self. They will be fundamental in whatever direction global education takes over the coming years.

One way of getting a purchase on the issues here is to recall some words of Ernst Toller's. Toller was born in 1893 near Bromberg, East Prussia (now Bydgoszcz in central Poland). He volunteered for military service in 1914, spent thirteen months on the Western Front, was discharged on grounds of ill health, was in hospital, studied at Munich and Heidelberg universities, became involved in socialist and secessionist politics in Bavaria, and from 1919 till 1924 was in prison. Whilst in prison he wrote poetry and plays and also a number of remarkable letters, reflecting on German and pan-European political and economic issues. In one letter he mused about patriotism, and about national, cultural and personal identity:

The words 'I am proud to be a German' or 'I am proud to be a Jew' sound ineffably stupid to me. As well say, 'I am proud to have brown eyes' ... Pride and love are not the same thing, and if I were asked where I belonged I would answer that a Jewish mother had borne me, that Germany had nourished me, that Europe had formed me, that my home was the earth, and the world my fatherland.[3]

At first sight, Toller's identity may appear much more complex than that of most people! But actually all of us experience analogous tensions and opportunities, for we are all of us pulled by our heritages and belongings in a range of different and contrary directions. Toller's essential distinction is between love and belonging on the one hand and what he calls pride on the other. He has known and enjoyed multiple sources of nourishment, support and formation, he says, and therefore feels multiple loves, gratitudes, obligations and loyalties — he has multiple belongings, formed from multiple dependencies. Some of these sources of nourishment and feelings of belonging are to do with his immediate family, and the cultural and religious tradition to which his immediate family belongs. Others are much larger and more amorphous but to evoke their power. Toller uses metaphors from close family life, parenting and being parented: 'motherland', 'fatherland'.

But whether immediate or amorphous, each source of nourishment is itself multiple, and loyalty to it risks being merely proud, merely parochial, uncritical and unreflecting. This is the situation for all of us, regardless of our particular rootedness in space, culture and generation. All people need an upbringing and education which will (a) help them to sort out their various loves and loyalties, and to hold them in balance and (b) enable them to make judgements, with regard to any one love or loyalty, about what they want to retain and absorb from the heritages to which they have been born and what they want to resist in them, or downright to reject. There are many practical and significant implications here for curriculum planning and delivery in the world studies field.

The handbook for teachers *Equality Assurance in Schools*, (Runnymede Trust, 1992) compiled through a lengthy process of consultation with teachers in 1991/ 1992, put forward the proposition that all pupils and students in schools (and all their teachers too, for that matter) need a sense of personal, ethnic and cultural identity which has three separate but interacting components.[4] Identity needs to be:

☐ confident, strong and self-affirming, as distinct from uncertain, ashamed or insecure;

☐ open to change, choice and development, as distinct from being dogmatic, rigid and opinionated;

☐ receptive and generous towards other identities, and prepared to learn from them, as distinct from feeling threatened and hostile, and wishing to exclude or to be separate.

To be developing as a world citizen, so far as sentiments and loyalties are concerned, is to be moving in these three ways. The 'terrestrial teacher', to recall again Jim Henderson's term, has this threefold sense of identity, and aims and works to develop such an identity in children and young people. Jim did not doubt that he was asking a lot. Terrestrial teachers, he said:

> must be able to manage a double loyalty, to their own local community with its particular needs and beliefs and to that supralocal, supranational, one world, without the orderly functioning of which no local community can any longer survive. Sometimes this effort will lead to their discomfort and even to their professional and personal martyrdom, but for this they must be prepared — it should be part of their training (Henderson, 1968).

The fourth component of citizenship is to do with political literacy and skill. It involves having sufficient knowledge about the political situations in which one takes part and sufficient competence in advocacy and mobilisation to defend and pursue one's interests. Increasingly political literacy has to be exercised not only in national politics but in subnational, transnational and supranational contexts also. This is the single most important assertion which the world studies movement has always made. It is emphasised time and again, implicitly as well as explicitly, throughout the pages of this book.

Global and local

Also, however, a recurring thread through this book is the need to hold in balance global and local, and personal and political. The four components of citizenship, for example, exist actually or potentially in a great range of contexts and situations. In local and personal affairs, as also in all other places and spaces, there is the choice — easy enough to state, but never easy to make or sustain — between force and debate. In global and political affairs, as also closer to home, we have to carry on hoping and persevering. Everywhere, in the tiniest of fleeting moments as well as in mighty and historic events, we human beings have a talent for doing the right thing at the wrong time, and the wrong thing at the right one. Jim Henderson once quoted Albert Camus on all this, recalling a magazine article which Camus had published in April 1940. The article had foreseen that in fifty years time Camus's grandchildren would be no closer to a sense of world citizenship than were most of his contemporaries as a new world war started around them. Therefore the task in the present, Camus said:

> is that some of us should take on the job of keeping alive, through the apocalyptic historical vista which stretches before us, a modest thoughtfulness which, without pretending to solve everything, will constantly be prepared to give some human meaning to everyday life (Camus, A., 1940).

In everyday life as in the grandest forums and battlefields of all humanity, Camus urged, there is a choice between violence and friendly persuasion, and between despair and hope:

> Over the expanse of five continents throughout the coming years an endless struggle is going to be pursued between violence and friendly persuasion, a struggle in which — I grant — the former has a thousand times more chances of success than the latter. But I have always maintained that if they who base their hopes on human nature are fools they who give up in the face of circumstances are cowards. Henceforth, the only honourable course will be to stake everything on a formidable gamble: that words are more powerful than munitions (Camus, A., 1940).

As terrestrial teachers strive to make that gamble, maintaining a modest thoughtfulness in local affairs as in global, and in personal as in political, one thing they need is to treasure the specific, the tiny, the one and only: this child, this moment, this place, this immediate local history and that person, that life, that life-work, that set of historical and cultural conditions in which a life and its work unfolded. So for example (and he himself, it is important to recall, would not have wished to be remembered in a context such as this other than as an example), it is fitting to name and honour James L. Henderson, 4 July 1910-19 April 1986. To name and honour one terrestrial teacher is to affirm the significance and dignity of all, their role and their worth as one and only individuals, in the overall global field.

Notes

1. 'The Terrestrial Teacher' is the title of a chapter in Henderson (1968).

2. For example, Henderson set up the World Studies Project in 1972, through his involvement with the One World Trust, itself an offshoot of the All-Party Parliamentary Group for World Government. There was unbroken continuity from this project of the early 1970s into the World Studies 8-13 project of the early 1980s. Henderson and the One World Trust assisted the world studies syllabus in the 1970s at Groby School, Leicestershire, and this syllabus led in its turn to the establishment by David Selby of the Centre for Global Education (as it came to be called) at York.

3. Quotations in translation from Toller's Briefe aus dem Gefängnis (1935), including this one, were provided in the programme for his play, The Machine Wreckers, National Theatre, 1995.

CHAPTER 2

'Listen to the South': Creating Partnerships in Education

Jaya Graves

Background

I write as one who has been involved in bringing a Southern view into many different areas of education, including peace and environmental groups. Since 1992 I have been working with Southern Voices, a Manchester- based project committed to presenting Southern perspectives both on issues that are seen to be specific to the South and on those of global concern. This has involved contact and liaison with schools, universities, community organisations, development agencies and development education centres; and facilitating processes through which people of the South and North can engage in fruitful and meaningful exchange. I have trained as a Waldorf teacher, using Rudolf Steiner methodology, so I have experience of working with children as well as adults. In this chapter, I wish to share my own perspectives as an educator, campaigner and 'animateur'; as well as a Southern person living and working in Britain.

The vision

My brief for this book was to develop a rationale for involving Southern people in Teacher Training. This has not been an easy piece of writing to get into. Some of this is due to a reluctance to repeat, again, what so many of us have been saying over and over, in so many different spheres for so many years. And because writing a rationale seems like a lapse into the paternalism so often apparent in the 'expert' syndrome of the 'development world'. However, since we have been saying these things over many years, it must mean either that the reasons are not self-evident or that there is a reluctance to implement what is never disputed in principle — a people's right to speak for themselves. There are implications to this acknowledgement. It means power sharing — in whatever area of work we are involved in. Sharing power means releasing some that we have accumulated for ourselves, whether as resources, 'knowhow', capital or information. Sharing power means less power for oneself.

Perhaps the best point of entry is to establish what I would hope for in a classroom, as a mother and a human being. (This of course is a reflection of the world I would like for *all* people. It also defines why Southern people need to be involved in classroom activities.) Such a classroom would be a place where diversity is not just accepted but celebrated as an essential part of our collective heritage, as wealth; where young people are encouraged to explore differences with openness, interest and excitement; where neither fear nor superiority is the touchstone of self definition; where divergent views and voices are heard with respect and without fear or pain; and where racism dies because in such a context it becomes irrelevant and ridiculous. This prevailing ethos, whether there is agreement or differences, for there will be both, will create a dynamic interaction where all learn, change and grow, including teachers and teacher educators. I would like a classroom to be a place where we do not kill curiosity and are not afraid of discussion and challenge; where children are stretched but not broken; where energy does not degenerate into aggression; where openness does not become power politics and marginalisation.

As all this runs contrary to the society we live in, such a classroom is not easy to achieve. But being an educator has never been easy, not in any age nor in any country — in some countries teachers can be harassed, imprisoned or even killed. What I'm writing is a vision statement. I feel that such a vision is essential, at a time and in a region where racism is increasing and we goose-step towards the millennium even as the long history of European exploitation returns to haunt the children of the exploiters. These phenomena are two sides of the same coin. It follows that those who teach in my ideal classroom must have certain skills, qualities and preparation. Facilitating the acquisition of these skills is the task of those who train our future teachers.

One question which may follow is, 'Why and how can the involvement of Southern people and Southern perspectives facilitate such preparation?' But since mine is not a utilitarian approach, I would ask first: '*Why* is there so little involvement of Southern people in many areas of work which are directly to do with *us*?' In reality there is a lack of plurality in the voices heard and faces seen in virtually all educational circles at every level. How many Black or Southern people are present at the conferences held, for example, by the Development Education Association, the Geographical Association, the World Studies conferences and a whole range of other similar events? How many Black or Southern people are there at policy-making level in these, and other relevant organisations?

Southern people would enrich ITE because Global Education//World Studies/ Development Education is part of every teacher's task. Implicit in each of the three terms above is the concept of inclusiveness — that the views and voices of many peoples are involved in each learning situation. Clearly this must include Southerners. If 'global' is really to mean inclusive, outreach and contact with these groups and individuals has to be incorporated as part of a job description for those who are involved in such work and/or organising these events. The same principles apply to those who organise teacher training courses. And we are speaking not only of a Southern presence in these forums but about making these views integral to the process.

There are powerful reasons for this. More and more UK citizens of non-British origin are complaining about the lack of material their children can identify with in our schools. Children themselves complain about it. And other children become strangers to their own parents. I recognise that this is Britain and that our particular 'cultures' cannot be retained as they are in our native lands. Culture is, in any case, a dynamic movement. The issue is exclusiveness; an educational approach where there is one 'norm' and all else is rendered the 'other': an 'other' defined as deviant or too difficult to understand, instead of accepted as merely different. There is little History or Geography or Literature in mainstream education, that tells our stories in our own voices, our own words. Our art, our songs and struggles are quarantined in 'ethnicity', our ancestors robbed of vibrancy and power and allocated no more than a few quotations, even though there is considerable first-hand material in print and available. There is a past that is shared by Black British and Southern people which all our children need to explore through the words of many writers in order to engage in an exchange that is honest. History has been whitewashed for long enough.

There is also the present, the reality we live in now, which has very much to do with the past. But so many people are afraid of looking at this, preferring to see a set of dates; a series of events rather than a process by way of which we arrive where we are now. The 'now' has become the domain of the 'experts', who have homogenised our diversity and called it the 'developing world'. But each 'developing' country has its own particular story and it is best told by the people who live there. Many of us have long argued that the real 'experts' are those who live the lives; who are emotionally as well as intellectually engaged with the issues/subject matter/country concerned. If you are serious about the 'wholeness' of education, then Southern people have to be involved in it in a way that is mutually satisfying and where quality is not sacrificed to the hoary old chestnuts *no time, no money, don't know any, I may give offence* (see below).

We are told that this is a 'multicultural' society. What traits does such a society possess? (There is a debate going on about the implications of the terms 'multicultural', 'anti-racist' and 'intercultural' which is beyond the scope of this paper). This book is concerned with the qualities and skills of the people who teach in its schools. These people need the ability and willingness to suspend a given cultural conditioning; to enter into the experience of *different* cultures and peoples; to engage with the magic and fear of difference and know that this enriches our lives.

We cannot overturn our cultural conditioning just by 'learning about', which is a passive and one-way process that denies the heartbeat of a culture and turns it into a 'thing' to be witnessed or bought. To enter into a culture, even briefly, means a dynamic engagement; perhaps a suspension of existing attitudes and assumptions. It is perhaps easier for people to pay lip service to such engagement than to practice it. Recently this was demonstrated to me at a conference for educators which had as a theme the question of culture 'One world or many worlds — looking at cultures and development'. Yet even here, people who were willing and apparently open to exploring the experience of being inside different cultures showed a resistance to facing up to the explicit violence in a poem presented by a Kenyan dramatist. This could be interpreted as unwillingness to engage with the violence inherent in all societies (including Britain) and/or unwillingness to give up a simple and idealised image of the rural South.

There are cultures where violence may be explicit and on the streets, unlike the British variety which is structural and insidious. If I get spat on in the street that is explicit violence. The British variety seldom immediately erupts in riot but it can, and has, done so. If teachers (along with others) will not, or cannot, identify the active presence of violence in this society, how can we teach children about non-violence, justice and peace? In order to teach in a multicultural society we must be willing to enter into someone's else's reality. It must be part of the trainer's task to prepare teachers for this kind of engagement. These things are urgent, not just for those of us who are on the receiving end of racism but for everyone. What kind of a society do we want to live in? Contact with people from different cultures facilitates a process of understanding and joy in our diversity which is our wealth. But such interaction must take place with respect and dignity.

Development Education, practised as popular education in most Southern contexts, requires that the practitioners attempt to see their own place and role in the processes under scrutiny. Such awareness can lead to internal change. This is education for self-development, where internal transformation is integral to the external processes of change. Thus in order to be truly global, teachers must go beyond a kind of tolerant 'multiculturalism' and be able to examine the complexities and paradoxes that are present in all human societies and understand the violence embedded in racism and post-colonial history. Student teachers need to locate themselves in a process of self-examination with regard to their own attitudes and values and engage in a critical assessment of their country's colonial past and its current involvement in exploitation of the South. I am not seeking to impose guilt on the present generation for the actions of their forebears but arguing that we are all required to take responsibility for where and who we are. When we truly do this, the ensuing changes in our own lives position us within the wider process of change.

Involving Southern colleagues in ITE sessions

For the last four years, Southern Voices has been involved with Development Education, in the widest sense. This has included classroom work and workshops with teachers and student teachers. What follows is based on that experience. We believe that the emphasis should be as much on 'learning from/with/through', as on 'learning about'. Three principles underpin much of the work of the Project: *mutuality, engagement* and *willingness to change.* Without these principles learning cannot take place. Our goal is not to provide an exotic experience — what a colleague once called 'educational tourism'. We are concerned with the kind of contact between Southern and Northern people which helps to break down stereotypes and inaccurate images and facilitates understanding.

Working Together

There are many strands to this work: here I am concerned with only two. One has to do with quality — ie *in what manner'* and the other relates to method — ie *'how/where can we find?'*

There are two basic requirements. One is **thorough preparation** before the first meeting. This is essential, particularly if there has been little previous contact. It is important to be clear about what is expected and what is being offered on both sides; to spend time over a contact, especially in the beginning, to nurture it, to build a relationship where any misunderstandings, (which are much dreaded) can be sorted out. The second requirement is **evaluation**, which must

be built into any meeting so that it is possible to learn from the experience for the future.

Some key considerations:

☐ *Language differences*: Southern people are not native English speakers — English may be a third, fourth or fifth language. Monolingual student teachers must be prepared to take time and make an effort to understand.

☐ *Differences in style*: We may not come directly to the point as is the usual practice here. Southerners will discuss through anecdote, stories and example. We may let things unravel in a much more leisurely way (unless we have been here for many years), as a means of developing a relationship with the audience.

☐ *Relationship to time*: Punctuality is not always possible or prioritised in many Southern countries. There are practical and cultural reasons for this, eg in the South transport can be unpredictable; access to phones difficult; the demands of interpersonal relationships are important. This produces a different framework in relationship to time which can create considerable misunderstandings in societies where time is measured precisely. Both parties need to be clear about expectations and problems.

☐ *Human interaction*: In most Southern countries a visitor would be received with interest and respect. This may not always be the case in this country. It is not my purpose to comment on these differences here, but it may be interesting for you to consider.

☐ *Representation.* One Southern person is not a 'representative' of 'the South' any more than a British person can be a representative for all of Europe or even the part of Britain in which they live. On the other hand, we do have certain shared experiences which give those of us who become involved in projects like Southern Voices a common purpose. It is important to hear a plurality of voices and views — which is true of most learning.

Southern Voices also does its own preparation with visitors. We warn visitors to expect certain differences. We talk about the pressure on teachers, timekeeping, about the social aspect: unfortunately racism has to be openly considered in advance. If you are working with people who have come recently to this country, you may need to brief them yourself or find someone who will. If you are working with settlers or long-term residents, there may be different issues to deal with. But there obviously needs to be preparation on both sides.

Making contact

Returning to the *how/where* question, Southerners are not thin on the ground in this country but it seems to be difficult for many people to make contact with us! Yet there are some simple things that can be done. Most towns in the UK have people with international connections living in their midst: students, settlers, refugees, long-term visitors. You can contact solidarity groups, university tutors (if you are based in a university there may be people on your doorstep), community groups. It is also valuable to use informal channels of contact like social occasions, commemoration days, celebrations, festivals.

Learning is a continual and two-way process so go to the courses and events planned by Black and Southern people, which operate in most large cities and towns. There are also materials (educational, artistic) produced by Black and Southern people, with which teachers and teacher educators need to become familiar.

ITE institutions need to develop communication with groups and people in their particular community. It is the *local* contact that can be developed into a sustainable process; an ongoing process of mutual learning and enrichment; something that can work, like a yeast, for change in the whole community. This may not be easy: it may take some time in the first instance, but if we are serious about an inclusive education we must make the effort. People are not invisible. Material and resources are available.

An ongoing relationship may be uncomfortable at times. Perhaps there is a deeper resistance than most people are prepared to recognise. It may have to do with looking at one's own attitudes and assumptions and the consequences of this internal enquiry. Seeing our own involvement in the chain of oppression is never easy, and nor is sharing power. This applies to people of the South as well as the North. Examining the processes through which we arrive at the present means not only examining the nation state, the structures and institutions which maintain the status quo, but also a self-examination that may be painful.

Conclusion

The teacher's task must be to encourage the child to explore and discover the excitement of his/her own inheritance, for we belong to the world and the world to us. And if some part of it is a bit strange to us, all the more reason for respectful exposure. In the long run it is the UK that has more to gain by involving Southerners in teacher training, the classroom or anywhere else. I have identified some of the benefits in this chapter, most of which have to do with credibility and authenticity within the learning environment. Yet for me one advantage stands out which is more important than any other, although it may not be recognised as such. This has to do with values. In many Southern cultures the location of value is not in things (as is increasingly the case in Britain) but in relationships: between individuals, within the family, in the community and between human beings and their natural and cultural environments. It is the breakdown of these relationships that creates so many of the problems prevalent in Northern societies. I recognise that this may be changing in certain levels in some Southern countries, but such values are still generally widespread.

Teachers will *always* have considerable impact on the children they teach, so those responsible for the training of teachers have the possibility of great influence on the generation to come. This is not something to approach lightly and needs constant reappraisal. Children can be, and are, taught a lot of facts and figures. They may be taught about people and countries, about the climate in India, the life expectancy in Kenya, dates of certain wars. Even about the lives people live — school children with no books, people on the streets, hospitals without medicines. But how do we nurture the curiosity and concern which is the natural condition of children? The legacy of school should be a mind that is flexible and mobile, yet centred, that knows we have to continue to change and grow, an ability to take the necessary risks without being foolish or thoughtless. If our children leave school like this then we are beginning to get something right.

Acknowledgements

This chapter is the result of many discussions with many friends and colleagues, and particularly Ahmed El Hassan, Opiyo Mumma, Sheela Hammond, Maryam Yassin, and Miriam Steiner.

CHAPTER 3

'I prefer to see myself as a Global Citizen': How student teachers can learn to teach for justice

Miriam Steiner

This chapter examines what it means to be a global teacher, the approaches to teaching and learning this entails and the role of initial teacher education in developing the understanding and commitments needed to create a more just world. I start from some recent research in which student teachers explored what they understand by citizenship and the place they feel it has in education. The title of this chapter and the statements in italics below are their words. This research underlined for me how important it is for student teachers to have the opportunity to explore global issues in their courses and to develop the wider understanding of what it means to be a global teacher.

Student teachers thinking about the meaning of citizenship

'I'd like to know what the distinction is between being a British or a global citizen.'

As part of our membership of a European education group, a colleague and I at Manchester Metropolitan University (MMU) developed a teaching module on the theme of citizenship which could be used by any member of the group, irrespective of specific local/national programmes of initial teacher education (ITE) (Steiner and Voiels, 1995).[1] We started from the belief that most teachers come to teaching with an inner vision of what constitutes a 'good society' and therefore are also operating with some definition of what it means to be a citizen. We were curious about how student teachers define citizenship in the abstract, and European citizenship in particular. We also wanted to know what they understand by concepts such as *democracy, human rights, social justice* and *global responsibility* and how they relate these to citizenship. Finally, we wanted to discuss with them the implications these personal meanings might or should have for their *practice* of teaching and for their future *role* as teachers.

The groups of undergraduate third year students in Manchester, Exeter and Utrecht, Holland who used our module shared broadly similar views: they regarded *rights* as the corner-stone of citizenship; they wrestled enthusiastically with defining political concepts and they decided that multicultural curricula, taught in classrooms based on shared respect and cooperation and using student-centred approaches, are the best means of teaching for citizenship(Steiner and Voiels, 1995).

This chapter discusses why it is important in ITE courses to have a deeper commitment to exploring the implications of citizenship at both the local and global level, than merely making space within the crowded ITE curriculum for a squashed one and a half hour session on 'The meanings of the cross-curricular theme of Citizenship and how to fit it into your planning and teaching'. Anyone learning to be a teacher should have the right and the duty to reflect upon and discuss these broad concepts so that they can become a 'global teacher'.

Student teachers addressing the defining principles of global citizenship

'There is a danger that this is a narrow view of citizenship — concentrating on our country and Europe — not a world perspective' (Dutch student).

When we asked the students in what ways they thought that '..the activities of being a citizen are underpinned by principles such as democracy, social justice, global responsibility and respect for human rights', the majority ruefully admitted that they had rarely thought about the meaning of these terms, and that their educational experiences had generally not prepared them to deal with abstract concepts (see Huckle, 1989). We appreciate that several dilemmas lie at the heart of asking student teachers our question. By their nature, these concepts are complex and their meanings contestable. Also, few ITE students have ever had formal teaching about political concepts and few opportunities within their courses to consider the meaning of these terms (see also Campbell and Davies, 1995).

Should the lack of experience in political education matter more to ITE students than any other undergraduates? If ITE is to produce the 'professional who can be a significant influence in a democratic and ethical society' (MMU, 1995), then its curriculum should be concerned with moral deliberation about local and global society as well as learning technique and subject content. If an 'ethical society' is one that recognises and addresses conditions of inequality, then courses for student teachers need to help them develop clear understanding about these inequalities, how they can work to overcome their effects on individual pupils and avoid reproducing them in their practice or relationships with children (see inter alia Klein, 1994 [and Chapter 6 in this book]; Shah, [Chapter 7 in this book], Siraj- Blatchford in Verma, 1993; Verma, 1993).

Student teachers thinking about the teaching processes for citizenship

> 'Any curriculum which is solely based on 'national knowledge' could never effectively teach about democracy and human rights' (British student).

Our module on citizenship ends by asking the students how their professional practice could reflect the values of democracy, social justice, global responsibility and respect for human rights. The British and Dutch student groups decided that a multicultural and global curriculum was fundamental, one firmly based on student-centred active learning, in which 'respect for others' is the core attitude. They identified *communication, open-mindedness and listening* as the basic skills for citizenship. All were certain that they would need to teach about a range of world cultures in order for their pupils to begin to understand the key concepts of citizenship, democracy, human rights, social justice and global responsibility.

The student teachers were not unrealistic idealists: they were concerned about the level of emotional and intellectual maturity that would be required to deal with the issues of citizenship. They realised the main challenge for them was to enable children of any and every group to understand and appreciate the importance of these issues. When they discussed their future role as teachers and the ways in which they would create a classroom environment in which these principles could be experienced by their pupils, three necessities for good practice emerged: *appropriate teaching methodology*, with a strong preference for student centred learning; the *quality of relationships in the classroom* — between teachers and pupils and between members of the class; and the underlying *principles of teaching and learning* based on democratic classroom organisation.

It is clear that, for these students, teaching is an ethical endeavour. They intend to help their pupils understand not merely subject knowledge but also interpersonal values, multicultural, environmental and global issues. As their statements quoted earlier show, they are positioning themselves as global teachers.

The global teacher: high ideal or basic requirement for democratic societies?

This book starts from the premise that teachers must 'act local and think global' if they want to prepare their pupils for what will be increasingly complex lives in the global economy of the twenty first century. By a 'global teacher' I mean a teacher who

☐   is interested in and concerned

about events and movements in the local, national and global community;

☐ actively seeks to keep informed while also maintaining a sceptical stance towards her sources of information;

☐ takes up a principled stand, and supports others who do so, against injustice and inequalities relating to race, gender, class, physical or mental attributes, and to international systems of trade, finance and production;

☐ informs herself about environmental issues as they impact upon her community and on other communities and ecological systems globally;

☐ values democratic processes as the best means of bringing about positive change and engages in some form of social action to support her beliefs.

As a teacher, he will

☐ model democratic values of fairness, justice and equal respect;

☐ use a range of teaching styles which foster both individual development and group cooperation and enable students to make the best use of their differing learning styles;

☐ encourage his pupils/students — whether infants or in higher education — to take up a reflective and questioning position in relation to knowledge;

☐ teach the prescribed curriculum well and also about the other important things that are not laid down, to do with human rights, relationships, self-esteem and respect for diversity;

☐ be a critical educator, that is, maintain a balance between a resolute framework of basic values and a position of sceptical reflection on any set of given norms — social, economic, political, cultural, pedagogic.

Other educators also provide powerful definitions and models for the global teacher and critical educator, see inter alia, Clough and Holden, (Chapter 5 in this book), Giroux, 1989 and 1992; hooks, 1994; Pike and Selby, 1989; Steiner, 1993.

The reflective global teacher starts from a commitment to human rights. She enacts her principles in her classroom and school and bases her professional practice, choice of teaching resources and her wider life on her attachment to global concerns. She has a clear sense of the ends of education, ends which have social and moral implications. Her teaching would be inherently ethical because it would avoid '..merely acting as conduit for the knowledge and values of the powerful' (Apple in Liston and Zeichner, 1991). It would be actively and constantly attuned to enabling learners, even of nursery age, to develop their own thinking and to uncover the implicit beliefs and values they already hold.

Teaching for global citizenship: values to support the global teacher

Our students identified three components of being a teacher which they believe they must attend to if they are to teach for citizenship: *appropriate teaching methodology, the quality of relationships in the classroom,* and *principles of teaching and learning based on democratic classroom organisation.* How would a 'global teacher' approach these?

Teaching methodologies

1. Choosing starting points: the first step might be to identify approaches to teaching which:

   ☐ value personal experience and feelings as essential elements in the learning process and take on the 'epistemological challenge' (Weiner, 1994) this presents;

   ☐ engage with a range of critical and open-ended pedagogies that redefine the role of the teacher;

   ☐ set out to build community within the diversity and differences that exist in any place of learning.

A pedagogy is more than a set of techniques and activities: it entails a moral framework about the relationship between learner and teacher and between teaching activities and the learning process. Feminist and transformative pedagogies offer an excellent starting point in this task (see, inter alia, hooks, 1994; Weiler, 1991; Weiner, 1994). A global teacher will infuse theories of learning with deeper human values and question the traditional dualisms that underpin education.

> The project for teacher educators that I am recommending ...is neither so simplistic nor so impoverished as one that merely replaces an emphasis on head with one on hand, one on reason with one on feeling and emotion, one on separation of the self with one on connection to others, one on the productive purposes of society with one on its reproductive processes. It is a difficult project to carry out because it is possible to join together the two sides of the various Platonic dichotomies only if they are equally valued (Martin in Liston and Zeichner, op cit).

2. Becoming a critical teacher:

   ☐ The curriculum tends to reproduce social norms and values in an unquestioned form.

   ☐ Using active learning and discussion-based activities is not sufficient to develop socially critical thinkers: a global teacher also presents content which provides a fuller and clearer representation of the world.

Active learning techniques such as group discussions and problem-solving, role-plays, simulations and cooperative games are often used in global education because they help combine both thinking and feeling, group discussion and individual reflection. They are ideal vehicles for enquiry learning — creating situations in which pupils can formulate questions and find answers for themselves. 'The important goals of world studies focus on learning to learn, solving problems, clarifying values and making decisions' (Fisher and Hicks, 1985).

The global teacher realises that she must be alert to a range of moral and methodological issues that are related to these theories about learning styles and their associated techniques. In Chapter 10, Nigel Toye and Chris Rowley observe that 'Global Education is concerned with raising questions, yet often it raises instant answers too, answers which fail to involve children properly in dialogue' (p.92). John Huckle in his chapter challenges global educators from another perspective,

> Experiential learning offers a space to contest and re-construct world views and, like the new social movements, it appeals strongly to the new middle class. Its acknowledgement of the relativity of knowledge and the significance of identity and cultural politics are to be welcomed but without adequate attention to critical theory and emancipatory politics, experiential learning is unlikely to constitute critical pedagogy (p.36)

The global teacher will be sensitive to these tensions faced by educators aspiring to be both critical and committed in their values and, at the same time, transformative in their use of pedagogy and exercise of power. Everyday 'school knowledge' is problematic because it is infused with prevailing ideologies and social values. For example, in subjects such as English, the Humanities, Religious and Environmental Education, where discussion and empathy-based activities are common, teaching methods and content often fail to move children beyond empty play acting or harbouring unrealistic Utopian wishes. Uncritical forms of teaching give a ...

> depoliticised and dehumanised view of the world ... because the issues for resolution presented to students are posed within a pluralistic, consensus view of society which emphasises the equality of all values and opinions and ignores the maldistribution of wealth, status and power in society ... and the use of various forms of power ... (Huckle in Fien, 1992).

The global teacher will want to be self aware even if it means ending up adopting different stances on different issues. Richardson's four *Attitudes to the Status Quo: conforming, reforming, deforming and transforming* (Richardson 1990), is a useful checklist for the global teacher who is pursuing the goals of developing independent, critical thinkers whilst attending to socially transforming outcomes. *Reforming* thinkers like Lipman provide models to help develop 'higher order thinking': a fusion of creative and critical thinking (Lipman, 1991) and *transformers* such as Huckle (Huckle, Chapter 4 and 1995) alert us to ways of maintaining a critical detachment from power. Teachers who have a commitment to transforming society and work towards this goal, even within existing structures, will be creating its change.

Quality of relationships

☐ Learning for democracy and global citizenship is not solely about a course in civics, development education or critical pedagogies. It is about unlearning the patterns of subordination and dominance that pollute relationships between male and female, black and white, young and older.

You can only teach about justice and democracy by just and democratic means, to paraphrase Gandhi. But in attempting to make classrooms more democratic places modelling equality we must face up to a fundamental problem. Put at its simplest, few of us have experienced any real equality with others on a regular basis in our lives. From childhood we have developed within relationships of subordination to or dominance over others — within the family, amongst peers, at school and in other social settings. 'The extended dependence of children on adults creates for us from our earliest years a seemingly endless series of conflicts which challenge individuality and authenticity in the struggle to make ourselves acceptable in the eyes of others' (Whitaker 1995).

We see this operating in our system of educating the young when the teacher takes the role of 'superior', in imparting his knowledge to the 'lesser', the pupil. This relationship of unequal exchange (although teachers often state that they gain and learn from the fresh and uncluttered viewpoints of children), is one not merely of unequal power but also of unequal rights.

Overall, we have not found very good ways to carry out the central task: to foster the movement from unequal to equal. In childrearing and education we do not have an adequate theory or practice....We have a great deal of trouble in deciding on how many rights 'to allow' to the lesser party. We agonise about how much power the lesser party shall have. How much can the lesser person express or act on her or his perceptions when these definitely differ from those of the superior? Above all there is great difficulty in maintaining the conception of the lesser person *as a person of as much intrinsic worth as the superior* (Miller, 1976, italics in original).

Miller goes on to examine how our most fundamental learning of inequality, based on gender, starts in the family and continues in other daily experiences with reinforcement from the visual and print media. Our gender thus 'moulds the very ways we perceive and conceptualise' our relationship to power, over ourselves and others.

The global teacher operates with the inherent belief that if people are treated in a just and democratic way, they will be more alert to the lack of democracy and justice in the world. Global teachers can try to help children understand about stereotyping (eg 'caring' as female; using technology, thinking analytically, as male). This would begin to give children the skills and understanding to recognise and question the daily diet of messages of inequality which pervade society — about gender, race, size and age. For student teachers critical reflection on their own development is a way to re-experience and to reflect on what it felt like to be without power and without respect and to see how this can be redressed in their own classrooms.

Principles of teaching and learning

Styles of thinking and understanding:

☐ Our minds are capable of a variety of ways of processing learning; most people tend to favour one or two.

☐ Most school learning is geared towards the analytical and notational, handicapping those who learn best through other styles.

Pupil-centred active learning and a sensitivity to the complexities and ranges of learning styles have always been at the heart of global education (Richardson, 1979; Fisher and Hicks, 1985; Pike and Selby, 1989; Steiner, 1993; Whitaker, 1995; Brown, 1996). The main elements in this model are its holistic approach to how individuals learn and interact and a concern that real-life issues form part of their learning. It recognises the practical and moral truth that there's neither one way of being 'normal' nor a unique 'norm' of thought. As hooks writes, 'Most of us were taught in classrooms where styles of teaching reflected the notion of a single norm of thought and experience, which we were all encouraged to believe was a universal norm. This is as true for non-White as for White teachers' (hooks, 1993).

Every learning situation is composed of people operating with a variety of learning styles as well as culturally influenced perspectives (Pike and

Selby, 1989; see also Brighouse in the Foreword to this book and Gardiner, 1993). An optimum learning environment can be achieved for all learners if they are offered a balanced menu of teaching styles. Gardiner, who speaks of 'multiple intelligences', challenges the ways we organise learning:

> The problem is less a difficulty with school learning *per se* and more a problem in integrating the notational and conceptual knowledge featured in school with the robust forms of intuitive knowledge that have evolved spontaneously during the opening years of life. If we can find ways in which to help students synthesise their several forms of knowing, we should be in a position to educate students for understanding (Gardiner, 1993).

A global teacher would choose diverse ways of presenting information and plan a range of approaches, from individual study to deliberate use of structured cooperative and peer learning, so that more pupils could exercise their preferred styles. Also, since world studies deals with issues that are morally, economically and socially complex and controversial, we have to approach them from a range of different angles to promote more than superficial understanding.

Teaching for the Future

If school learning is about preparing children for the life they will live as adults, it also needs to attend to questions about the world in which this future will be lived. This means that the global teacher will think both about the short-term development of each child in his care and the longer term future of the world both will live in. This leads him to think about including 'Future Relevant Knowledge' (Tough, 1991) in what he teaches. As Hicks (1994) writes

> The purpose of 'education for the future' is to enable pupils to explore various scenarios which may emerge from current trends and to explore the implications of these. Once we realise that we cannot 'opt out' of the future, it takes on a radically new meaning. All actions and choices, including choices not to act or choose, have future consequences.

Even very young school children have distinct opinions about the futures that they might have: all too many start their schooling buoyant and leave passive and negative. The global teacher will enable pupils to explore their imagined and preferred scenarios. Gender plays a role here too as Hicks and Holden's research shows (Hicks and Holden, 1995). Boys rely on the 'technological fix' (which, paradoxically, they also fear will deny them meaningful jobs as adults) and girls, who put '..greater emphasis on people and relationships and less on technology...need to be able to engage confidently with technology at all levels' (ibid: p.107).

This may be true of teachers too: 'The problem is that modernist teachers are trying to teach post-modern kids', observes Erica McWilliam of Queensland University of Technology. She goes on to warn teachers not to be 'techno-paranoid' but to use information technology to develop critical thinking (*Times Educational Supplement*, 24 November, 1995).

The role of ITE

Being schooled is the one experience common to almost everybody in our society. Before they can move on to become teachers working for a more just society, student teachers need to reflect on what they themselves experienced as pupils: examine, analyse and share their own memories of schooling and emerge from the shell that many will have grown to protect themselves. Without shared critical reflection, all that new teachers will do is to reproduce their own experiences, and, even if these were happy, remain unable to meet the needs of this generation of pupils.

The student teachers described earlier, grappling enthusiastically with the abstract concepts of citizenship, demonstrate that preparing learners for global citizenship, at whatever level, also involves training in formal thinking, formal political education, and engaging with concepts. Student teachers need opportunities to spend more time in good exploratory discussion about 'big' ideas.

Institutions of higher education are responding to DfE 14/93 and other government decrees by restructuring courses, constructing their own competences and mission statements. To prepare teachers who will have a just and global vision such courses have to go beyond the thirty three competences specified — all of which are sound and most of which are 'technocratic'. Only the last relates to that extra ingredient required for a global teacher:

> Newly qualified teachers should have acquired in initial training the

necessary foundation to develop: vision, imagination, and critical awareness in educating their pupils (DFE 14/93 2.7.8).

Nick Clough and Cathie Holden in Chapter 5 offer us a powerful set of model competences for teacher educators preparing the global teacher.

The goals of knowing our values and valuing our knowing may well seem like another Everest for teacher educators, full of high ideals and inevitable crevasses.

> Progressive, holistic education, 'engaged pedagogy' is more demanding than conventional critical or feminist pedagogy. For, unlike those two teaching practices, it emphasises well-being. That means that teachers must be actively committed to a process of self-actualisation that promotes their own well-being if they are to teach in a manner that empowers students...a classroom is (not) diminished if students and professors regard one another as 'whole' human beings, striving not just for knowledge in books, but knowledge about how to live in the world (hooks, 1994).

It may appear to us that the professional pressures we grapple with daily may be reducing our energy and diminishing our enthusiasm for the tasks of being global citizens ourselves. Yet in the end, caring enough to cherish ourselves as well as our students and maintaining just and caring communities where we live and teach is the soundest practice for global teachers.

Note

1. Erasmus Curriculum Development ICP UK-95-2180/05: Education for Citizenship in a New Europe: learning democracy, social justice, global responsibility and respect for human rights.

CHAPTER 4

Globalisation, Postmodernity and Citizenship

John Huckle

This chapter argues that teacher education should introduce global citizenship as one of the grand theories or narratives which sustain modern development. The notion of citizenship has been periodically revived and students should consider to what extent its current revival can be attributed to accelerating globalisation and the emergence of new forms of social organisation and culture which are labelled postmodernity and postmodernism. Students should recognise that such developments can be turned in either positive or negative directions and that a constructive postmodernism now requires a reformulation of those models of democracy whereby global citizenship can be realised. This is likely to involve a re-assessment of liberalism and Marxism, a wider definition of politics, and the design and implementation of a multi-layered and multi-dimensional model of democracy which can enable people everywhere to engage in

ecologically and socially sustainable forms of development. The politics of culture and identity can be the key to motivating young people to become active and informed global citizens. Teacher education for global citizenship should pay greater attention to the ways in which recent developments in social and cultural theory have informed the theory and practice of socially critical pedagogy.

Modernity and citizenship

Modernity as a form of social organisation has its origins in the 16th century and its development was accelerated by the Enlightenment in the late 17th and early 18th century. Modernisation was to be realised by the systematic development of science and technology and their rational application to economic and social affairs. It involved industrialisation and the expansion of a global capitalist economy with a related division of labour; the consolidation of the centralised nation state together with the extension of bureaucratic forms of administration and liberal democratic forms of government; the formation of new social classes and increasingly complex patterns of social stratification; and a break with traditional worldviews and the adoption of a 'modern' or 'scientific' outlook. Grand theories or narratives of development, social emancipation, and citizenship shaped the rise of modernity, and education and schooling as modern institutions were often justified in terms of such goals.

Modernity brought a growing preoccupation with the nature and limits of political authority, law, rights and duties, and with the principle of autonomy which would shape their realisation (Held, 1994a). This principle suggests that individuals should be free and equal in the determination of the conditions of their own lives. That is, they should enjoy equal rights (and accordingly, equal obligations) in the specification of the framework which generates and limits the opportunities available to them, so long as they do not deploy this framework to negate the rights of others. The conditions of enactment of this principle determine the nature of democracy and citizenship and have been a continuing focus for political disagreement and conflict.

Liberalism ties liberty and equality to individualistic values and suggests that people are free and equal only to the extent that they can pursue and attempt to realise self-chosen ends and personal interests. The state should be restrained in the interest of individual freedoms and citizenship is essentially a matter of ensuring rights to personal freedoms

and access to justice via the courts (*civil citizenship*), and the right to vote in elections (*political citizenship*), in return for such obligations as respect for other people's rights and the authority of the state. Marxism, on the other hand, adopts collectivist values and questions whether liberty and equality can be realised by individuals left to their own devices in a 'free market' economy with a minimal state. It seeks a truly democratic economy, society and state, in the belief that only a fundamental re-organisation of modernity can ensure that the free development of each is compatible with the free development of all. In the twentieth century socialists in many countries promoted social citizenship or the right to a minimum standard of welfare and education to allow participation in society.

Specifying the conditions for enacting the principle of autonomy also involves specifying the nature of the community to which it should apply. Modern culture holds that the needs and interests of all human beings are universally similar and that the global community of humankind is the end or object of the highest moral endeavour. The theme of universal or global citizenship continues to shape the West's 'civilising' mission to much of the world and is reflected in both liberalism and Marxism, which look forward to the eventual emergence of a cosmopolitan world society after the removal of those structures, either the state or capitalism, which are seen to prevent the realisation of a global community based on liberty, justice and equality for all (Oliver and Heater, 1994).

Globalisation and postmodernity

Globalisation is a process whereby events, decisions and activities in one part of the world come to have significant consequences for individuals and communities in distant locations. Modernity entailed globalisation from the outset but since 1945 new technologies have allowed trans-national enterprises to accelerate the process by adopting new forms of corporate organisation which overcome frictions of distance (information technology), social organisation (standardised work methods), and culture (global media and consumerism). The 'post-war boom' from 1950 to the mid 1970s brought major changes in the scale, sophistication and interdependence of the world economy, and globalisation accelerated further in the 1980s and 1990s as capital sought to overcome supply and demand side crises and the governments of nation states sought to overcome legitimation crises through trans-national integration. The results of accelerating globalisation are profound. They lead some social theorists to claim that modernity has become exhausted and that we are entering a postmodern era characterised by new forms of social organisation, politics and culture.

According to these theorists (Harvey, 1989; Smart, 1993) the recent restructuring of the global economy has used the new technologies to obtain greater flexibility with respect to production, labour and markets, and has thereby quickened rates of innovation and capital circulation. The accompanying shift from Fordist development (based on mass production and consumption, routine labour processes and a social democratic mode of regulation) to post-Fordist development (characterised by flexible forms of economic organisation and production, more pluralistic lifestyles, and changed modes of regulation) has been facilitated by the economic and political liberalism of the New Right (Allen, 1992). It has brought a vast increase in the range of products and services potentially available to the consumer and has created new status and class divisions along with new interests and insecurities. In societies where the nature and availability of work have changed radically and the production of cultural products and services has assumed a new significance, the old politics related to production has declined and a new politics, focusing on issues of consumption and identity, has emerged.

The cultural impact of post-Fordism has been to produce new aesthetic, cultural and intellectual forms and practices, which are labelled postmodernist to distinguish them from the cultural styles and movements which dominated the modern era. Postmodernism revels in fragmentation, ephemerality and discontinuity; brings a new sensitivity to difference and subjectivity; replaces 'high-brow' culture with popular culture and consumerism; and suggests that there are no epistemological foundations or grand narratives via which all things can be connected, represented, or explained. While orthodox Marxists dismiss postmodernism as a cultural manifestation of disorganised capitalism (Lash and Urry, 1987) which encourages philosophical relativism and diverts attention from class struggle, post- Marxists seek a constructive postmodernism which acknowledges and corrects the mistakes of modern development and harnesses new political sensibilities to revised and more pluralistic forms of socialism's emancipatory narrative (Wainwright, 1994).

Constructive postmodernism represents modernism coming to terms with its limits. Social theorists, both feminist and green, provide many insights about how the excesses of modernism (for example its materialism, individualism, patriarchy, scientism, secularism and anthropocentrism) can be recognised and overcome. The decline of US hegemony, the continuing de-colonisation process in many parts of the world, the rise of the Asian tigers, the emergence of China, the increasing audibility of voices from the South, are just some of the many factors which challenge western modernity and mean that its central beliefs and values can no longer be claimed to be 'universal'.

Clearly if student teachers are critically to evaluate the extent and potential of the postmodern condition and understand how closely it is articulated with the processes of globalisation, their courses will need to be underpinned by contemporary social theory. Courses of teacher education should introduce the differing ways of theorising globalisation; help students to recognise its essentially contradictory or dialectical nature; examine its impact on education and schooling; and encourage speculation on where it may be leading. Giddens (1991), Beck (1992),

McGrew (1992) and Lash and Urry (1994) are indicative of relevant literature and many students will find reading them intellectually challenging. Accordingly, their studies need to be anchored in the kinds of realities brought to us monthly by the *New Internationalist* (for example Ellwood, 1993) and their tutors should continually encourage debate about the professional relevance of such ideas. They do, for example, help to explain the nature and politics of development and global education in the 1980s and set possible pointers for future curriculum development.

Rethinking the modern political community and citizenship

Globalisation compromises the competence, form, autonomy and legitimacy of the modern nation state and forces us to rethink our understanding of the political community and citizenship. At the same time as the nation state is threatened from above by growing global interdependence and the growth of international political institutions and agencies, it is also threatened from below by local groups, movements and nationalisms, seeking the devolution of power, greater self-management, and a broadening of politics to embrace new concerns. Nation states are increasingly too small to address the really big problems of life and too large to address local issues. They must nevertheless seek to maintain their legitimacy and such measures as citizens' charters and new curriculum guidelines for citizenship education are therefore to be expected (Oliver and Heater, 1994; Gilbert, 1995). These keep the principle of autonomy and its enactment on the agenda and remind us that they should be re-thought for postmodern or new times.

In Held's view (Held, 1994a, 1994b) such re-thinking entails a review of the strengths and weaknesses of liberalism and Marxism, a broadening of our conception of politics, and the design and implementation of a cosmopolitan model of democracy which is both multi-layered and multi-dimensional. Liberalism's scepticism regarding the abuse of political power complements Marxism's scepticism concerning the abuse of economic power and while liberalism's central failure is to see markets as powerless mechanisms of co-ordination, Marxism's central failure is to reduce political power to economic power and neglect the dangers of centralised political power and the need for accountability. Liberalism is too ready to equate politics with the narrow world of government while Marxism tends to marginalise issues that cannot, in the last analysis, be reduced to class related matters. The rise of the new social movements suggests that both have too narrow a view of politics and Held offers a wider vision in which politics becomes a universal dimension of human life:

> In my view, politics is about power, that is, it is about the capacity of social agents, agencies and institutions to maintain or transform their environment, social or physical. It is about the resources that underpin this capacity and about the forces that shape and influence its exercise. Accordingly, politics is a phenomenon found in and between all groups, institutions (formal and informal) and societies, cutting across public and private life. It is expressed in all the activities of co-operation, negotiation and struggle over the use and distribution of resources. It is involved in all the relations, institutions and structures which are implicated in the activities of production and reproduction in the life of societies. Politics creates and conditions all aspects of our lives and it is at the core of the development of problems in society and the collective modes of their resolution (Held, 1994a).

If politics is conceived in this way, then the design and implementation of models of democracy should provide all citizens with power to shape the processes of social production and reproduction affecting their lives. Globalisation means that democracy has to become a local, national, regional and transnational affair, with an expanding framework of democratic institutions and agencies regulating the ways we live together in what could be an increasingly diverse, yet just and peaceful world.

Held's cosmopolitan model of democracy includes multiple and overlapping networks of power within which all groups and associations are attributed rights of self-determination specified by a commitment to individual autonomy and a specific cluster of rights. These comprise rights within and across each network of (economic, political, social and cultural) power and constitute the basis of an empowering system of democratic international law. Law making and enforcement is developed at a variety of locations and levels with an expansion of the influence of regional and international courts. Legal principles delimit the form and scope of individual and collective action within the organisations and associations of state and civil society, and the principle of non-coercive relations governs the settlement of disputes. The overall collective priorities are the defence of self-determination, the creation of a common structure of action, and the preservation of the democratic good. These mean that social production and reproduction take place in ways which ensure ecologically and socially sustainable development.

There are other cosmopolitan or global models of democracy which student teachers might consider (for example Barnaby, 1988; IUCN/UNEP/WWF, 1991; Ekins, 1992; Swift, 1993). Preparation to teach in a global society should develop a knowledge and understanding of current world affairs (Segal, 1993), the nature and limitations of such international bodies as the European Union and the United Nations, and the potential for their reform or replacement by democratic alternatives. It should enable the envisioning of a truly new world order in which politics and civil society are revitalised and operate at many levels. Such studies risk remaining abstract and alienating, however, unless there is sufficient attention to cultural politics and socially critical pedagogy.

Cultural politics

Contemporary social theory suggests that globalisation challenges the existential foundations of people's lives and gives a new significance to cultural politics. Lash and Urry's account (1994) of the emerging economies of signs and space suggests, for example, that global information and communication structures are displacing other social structures as the prime determinants of social life. These structures erode previously existing meanings of objects and subjects, and the spatio- temporal context in which they are found, and prompt a growing number of people to take advantage of increased access to cultural products and competences to create their own meanings, monitor and organise their own individual life narratives, and attempt to reshape society itself.

Nowhere are these trends more apparent than in the popular and consumer cultures of the young. These are used to construct new and quickly changing identities and communities. In postmodern times cultural and identity politics appear far more real than the kinds of politics associated with the economy, the state, and civil society. Protests over the community charge, road construction and live animal exports reflect the appeal of cultural politics amongst the young and its power to build new alliances in changed times.

> Identity politics sees the socially-defined personal and interpersonal realms as the most important site of power relations ('the personal is political'), and its practitioners tend to focus more heavily on individual and group self-transformation than on engaging with the state...

... In identity politics the concern is much more for how people experience power relations in their everyday lives, and how their sense of themselves and their relations with others is given meaning. Taking political action, participating in the political process in all its diversity, becomes a matter of self-construction, reflection and expression (Gilbert, 1995).

Rob Gilbert (1995) argues that teachers should recognise cultural politics as a necessary aspect of citizenship education which holds the key to gaining young people's interest and motivating them towards democratic action. Interpreting and producing the meanings through which experience is represented and identities are formed, needs to become an important dimension of citizen's rights and a part of all people's education. Lessons on the political economy of culture can link cultural rights to the civic, political and social rights of conventional citizenship and to the expanded network of rights provided the global citizen by such cosmopolitan models of democracy as that outlined above. Radical environmentalism recognises the importance of cultural politics and expanded models of democracy and citizenship and the *What We Consume* module of the World Wide Fund for Nature's Global Environmental Education Programme (Huckle, 1988, 1993) demonstrates how such concerns can inform the development of a curriculum designed to promote global citizenship.

Critical pedagogy

Like other curriculum materials in development and environmental education, *What We Consume* seeks to promote a critical pedagogy through which teachers and pupils reflect and act on social alternatives in ways informed by critical theory and ideas. Edwards and Usher (1994) define critical pedagogy as:

> a broad and diverse field of theory and practice drawing on aspects of the modernist perspective of the later Frankfurt School, feminism, Freirean pedagogy, postcolonial discourse as well as postmodernism to construct a radical approach to education.

Student teachers clearly need a sound grasp of this diverse field since it offers a way of integrating constructive postmodernism with the more radical elements of modernist discourse. Giroux (1992) develops the concepts of border and postcolonial pedagogy in exploring how postmodernism's emphasis on diversity, contingency and cultural pluralism can be combined with modernism's concern for enlightenment and emancipation. Such pedagogy deconstructs authoritative voices, gives voice to those on the borders (the excluded and oppressed), and seeks to confront the Eurocentric, imperialistic and racist discourses of modernity in recognition of globalisation and multiculturalism. It acts as a vehicle for citizenship education which employs cultural politics to link abstract rights to everyday life and rejects definitions of community as the legitimating and unifying practices of a one-dimensional historical and cultural narrative.

Education as critical pedagogy or cultural politics is one response to the modern state's crisis of governability, legitimation and disillusionment. It offers an alternative to the authoritarian popularism and educational reforms of the New Right by providing a means of reformulating and extending citizenship in the ways outlined in this chapter. It is strongly reflected in James Lynch's advocacy and model of citizenship education for a multicultural society (Lynch, 1992) but has had too little influence on mainstream global and development education. Not only does this reflect an inadequate grasp of globalisation and social theory, it often embraces experiential learning in ways which may not realise its emancipatory potential.

Increased support for such learning reflects the changed modes of regulation in post-Fordist or postmodern society. Seduction largely replaces repression in the classroom and education's preoccupation with the cultivation of desire through experience partly replaces its preoccupation with the cultivation of reason and autonomy (Usher and Edwards, 1994). Experiential learning offers a space to contest and re-construct world views and, like the new social movements, it appeals strongly to the new middle class. Its acknowledgement of the relativity of knowledge and the significance of identity and cultural politics are to be welcomed but without adequate attention to critical theory and emancipatory politics, experiential learning is unlikely to constitute critical pedagogy.

A world still to be won

All this may seem rather abstract and distant from the everyday work of teacher educators. Professional voices have been marginalised or captured in the Right's reform of our work and there is less scope and encouragement for courses which incorporate critical theory and pedagogy. Nevertheless the radical development, environmental and citizenship education communities have managed to sustain and develop themselves in hard times. We now have theory and practice with which we can better meet the challenges of globalisation and postmodernity and so help to re-construct citizenship and the global order. Current trends do offer the prospect of more diverse, equitable and sustainable futures and if we hold our ground, the conditions in which we can make really significant advances will surely arise (Hill, 1991; Zeichner, 1993). Attempts to revive modernist forms of education in postmodern times are displaying mounting contradictions and along with other contradictions these will bring continuing change. We urgently need new kinds of teachers for new times and their ability to educate for global citizenship will be a critical factor in all our futures.

CHAPTER 5

Global Citizenship, Professional Competence and the Chocolate Cake

Nick Clough and Cathie Holden

Introduction

This chapter discusses the development of professional competences for the global teacher. Our intention is to provide a set of criteria and a framework for evaluation which can be used by those wishing to develop professional competence related to a global perspective in themselves or in others, that is teachers, university tutors and student teachers.

Our rationale draws on an overarching definition of the global teacher as one who can educate for citizenship:

> within a global context of human rights and social responsibilities contributing to the achievement of democratic values and behaviour in pluralist societies and in a culturally diverse world (Lynch, 1992).

Like Lynch we would argue that this education involves the development of personal consciousness and social participation at local, national and international levels. Such teaching not only reflects social and environmental features of the wider world outside the school but also aims to encourage participation within that world. Put another way, we maintain that the global teacher shares with the educator for the future two traditions identified by Hicks (1994):

> The first is the humanistic learner-centred tradition which focuses on the development and fulfilment of each individual. The second is concerned with building greater equality in society by highlighting and challenging existing inequalities of race, gender, class and disability.

The global teacher not only aims for high academic standards but also ensures that her classroom is run along democratic lines, that there is a multicultural and global dimension to her teaching, that issues of justice and fairness are raised when appropriate and that children feel they are being empowered as citizens of tomorrow.

The development of professional competences for such a global teacher may appear to be over-ambitious in a climate where resources and time available for initial teacher training are being diverted towards teaching and learning in the core subjects of the National Curriculum. However, a strengthening of the professional competence with respect to English and mathematics should not, in our view, be at the expense of the democratic fabric of our society. Indeed we would argue that the truly competent teacher needs to be proficient in teaching basic skills and also in preparing children for life in a pluralist society.

Legitimation

We do not have to look far for legitimation of this view. Section 1 of the Education Act 1988 requires that the curriculum should promote the spiritual, moral, social and cultural development of pupils at school and in society. This is now a focus for the inspection of primary initial teacher training where very good students are identified as showing evidence of 'vision, imagination and critical awareness in educating their pupils' (Ofsted, December 1994).

Within schools some teachers have responded to the challenge of Section 1 by ensuring permeation of the cross-curricular themes of citizenship, economic and industrial understanding, health and environmental education. The cross-curricular dimensions of

multicultural education, equal opportunities (gender) and personal, social and moral education have also provided encouragement for teachers to address wider social and political issues.

Within initial teacher education the promotion of vision, imagination and critical awareness has often been achieved through the development of reflective teaching. A recent survey of initial teacher training courses in England and Wales indicated that over 80% of them were based on a model of 'the reflective teacher' (Barrett et al 1992). The possible relationship between reflective teaching and the 'global' teacher has been described by Menter and Clough (1995). They trace the concept of the reflective teacher as an 'extended professional' from Dewey, to Schon (1983, 1987), to the more politicised versions developed by Zeichner (1981/2) and Giroux (1988). They conclude that:

> One of the clearest articulations of what is meant by reflective teaching is offered by Pollard and Tann (1987) who emphasise the importance for teachers of aims as well as means and who invoke the Universal Declaration of Human Rights and the European Convention on Human Rights and describe the key attitudes of a reflective teacher as open-mindedness, wholeheartedness and responsibility. These of course are very much traditional values within liberal democracies and within humanistic liberal education.

The UK is a signatory to the Council of Europe's recommendations to member states on teaching and learning about human rights which legitimates a concern to include the development of such reflective professional qualities within initial teacher education (Starkey, 1991).

However, there has been an observable shift away from direct references to such values in a number of recent official statements. Until 1993, the criteria for teacher education, which rested with the Council for Accreditation for Teacher Education, made explicit that the professional development of student teachers should include references to multicultural education and controversial issues. These criteria have now been replaced within the DfE circular 14/93 whose competences emphasise professional development related to the processes of assessing, recording and reporting children's achievements within a subject-based curriculum. Furthermore, the revised National Curriculum, introduced in 1995, makes no reference to the cross- curricular themes or dimensions which had provided opportunities and encouragement for teachers to address wider social and political issues. The emphasis is on the programmes of study in each separate subject area, with, in theory, more time available for schools to follow their own areas of interest.

While the Council of Europe and many professional educators might agree on the need for new teachers to be trained as global teachers, and while the Education Reform Act (1988) would imply the need for this, the new proposals for training teachers appear to put this at risk. If the global perspective is not to be lost, it must be embedded in the new competency-based approach to teacher training, used by both staff and students in faculties of education and the teachers who have increasing responsibilities for training in schools. The basis for such global education must now be located in the National Curriculum programmes of study as well as being taught as cross-curricular themes.

Professional competences for the global classroom

The introduction of a competency-based approach in initial teacher education is relatively new, arising out of the influence of National Vocational Qualifications. The requirement of DFE Circular 14/93 that students should 'focus on the competences of teaching throughout the whole period of initial training' raises serious issues for the education of the global teacher if competences are seen as skills to be learnt rather than as adopting a questioning and reflective approach. In the debate about the nature and value of competences Whitty and Willmott (1991) warn of the danger of over-emphasis on skills and techniques, arguing that 'what informs performance is as important as performance itself... the whole is more than the sum of the parts'. They identify two major approaches to competences:

— competence characterised as an ability to perform a task satisfactorily, the task being clearly defined and the criteria of success being set out alongside;

— competence characterised as wider than this, encompassing intellectual, cognitive and attitudinal dimensions, as well as performance; in this model, neither competences or the criteria for achievement are so readily susceptible to sharp and discrete identification.

They indicate that some competences are person-related and some task-related, and that statements of competences must look to combine the two; they must 'encompass the underpinning knowledge and understanding required for effective performance'. Furlong (1992) also warns of the dangers of a focus on competences providing too simplistic an approach. He cites Walker (1992), who maintains that 'teaching is more than a technology; it is a moral practice whose successful performance depends on a structure of competence in which abilities are not isolated discrete elements but are linked together structurally'. Teaching, Furlong concludes, is both 'multi-faceted and culture dependent'.

Our rationale is developed from this wider understanding of competences. Currently professional competences fall into the broad categories of curriculum content, planning and assessment, teaching strategies and further professional development. The characteristics of a list of professional competences which provides for the development of global teachers are significantly different although not incompatible. A reflective approach to teaching and learning is fundamental to both, with the global teacher being aware of the relationship between children's learning and broader societal and environmental factors. Thus a concern for social justice would be reflected in practice which not only promotes high academic standards but also promotes respect for cultural diversity and shared decision making. Likewise a concern for a sustainable future would necessitate purposeful application of subject knowledge to address such concerns.

Figure 1 illustrates the dynamics of the relationship between self, society and the activity of teaching and learning. It emphasises that for the teacher who is concerned with democracy, rights, responsibilities and justice, the processes of personal and professional development are inseparable. It also demonstrates how the 'ethos' of the classroom — itself the object of concern and scrutiny — is not an isolated phenomenon but a product of social interaction which resonates from and into the wider world. It signals that the professionally competent teacher needs to research, understand and care about the predicaments and controversies of the communities and environments of the wider world.

We have identified three key areas in defining further the competences which relate to the development of such a global teacher. Our focus on controversial issues and democratic processes draws on both Lynch and Furlong (op cit). The values the teacher brings, the pedagogical approach she takes and the application of a global perspective in the selection of appropriate subject matter lie at the heart of the global teacher. Each competence is described in terms of observable behaviours and can be used

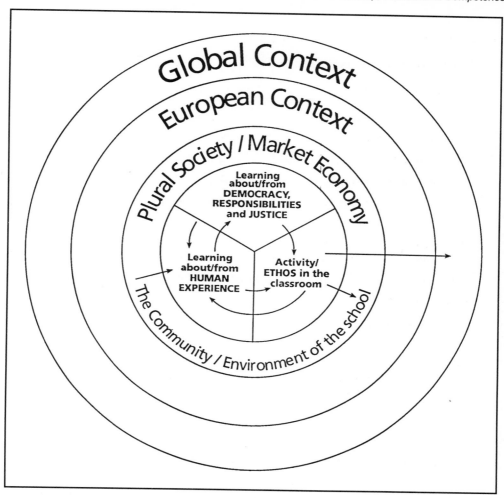

Figure 1: This diagram is adapted from a figure in Kimber, D., Clough, N., M., Harnett, P., Menter, I., and Newman, P. (1995)

for evaluating the work of others or for self evaluation. Following Whitty and Willmott (op cit) we have divided the competences into *person-related*, where the focus of the action is the teacher's own performance, and *task-related*, where action is required of the children.

Case studies: competences for the global teacher

The case studies which follow illustrate how BA/BSc (Hons) QTS student teachers responded to such competences. The first involved collaborative research drawing on a range of subject disciplines for a presentation, focusing on a topic related

Competences required of the global teacher

Promotion of democratic processes

Person-related:

- [ ] actively listening to children in the classroom;
- [ ] acknowledging the views of children and drawing on their experiences;
- [ ] responding to such observations through subsequent planning;
- [ ] evaluating own contribution to discussion;
- [ ] awareness of gender issues and of challenges facing children with special educational needs;
- [ ] awareness of cultural stereotyping and the challenges facing children from ethnic minority backgrounds;
- [ ] taking positive action to ensure equal access to learning for all pupils.

Task-related:

- [ ] encouraging children to listen to each other, to take turns and take responsibility;
- [ ] facilitating collaborative group work and democratic decision making;
- [ ] using new formats of decision making which the children suggest;
- [ ] introducing children to an understanding of rights and responsibilities (eg *encouraging children to relate these to the classroom and playground*) ;
- [ ] encouraging children to participate democratically in the community and in the wider world;
- [ ] encouraging children to think about their rights and responsibilities in the future;
- [ ] encouraging children to take justice and equality as starting points for decision making;
- [ ] encouraging independent learning.

Management of controversial issues

Person-related:

- [ ] awareness of own viewpoint;
- [ ] sensitivity to viewpoints of children in the classroom;
- [ ] sensitivity to differing experiences (social and cultural) of children;
- [ ] awareness of viewpoint in different sources of information;
- [ ] critical use of textbooks and other learning materials;
- [ ] awareness of rights of others and the need to promote respect for those rights;

Task-related:

- ☐ offering opportunities for children to detect partiality and viewpoint (eg *through examining different resources, role-play, simulation games*);

- ☐ encouraging children to acknowledge others' viewpoints and to defend or modify their own in the light of new evidence;

- ☐ promoting an awareness in children that many areas have the potential for controversy and that there are many perspectives to any one issue;

- ☐ promoting an understanding that justice, equality and human rights are basic tenets of a democratic society and central to many controversies.

Application of subject knowledge

Person-related:

- ☐ knowledge of subject and understanding of the nature of enquiries in that subject;

- ☐ applying own subject knowledge to the themes of citizenship, environment and economics; understanding of cross-curricular potential within these themes;

- ☐ sensitivity to the need to raise awareness of global issues in all subjects;

- ☐ understanding that possibilities to incorporate a global dimension can be found in all subjects;

- ☐ provision of wide range of teaching/learning materials which reflect this;

- ☐ design of own relevant materials which develop children's subject knowledge and understanding of global citizenship.

Task-related:

- ☐ managing enquiries by children into these themes using approaches from the different subject disciplines;

- ☐ drawing personal responses from children related to such enquiries.

to global citizenship in a changing world and to National Curriculum humanities work. There then follows an example of a student planning and teaching a lesson related to this topic with children in KS2. The second case study follows a student's lesson on world maps.

Case Study One
Global trade and the chocolate cake: a collaborative presentation to other students

One group's presentation on 'The Chocolate Trade' included consideration of:

☐ historical perspectives, including the history of eating and drinking chocolate and the history of Cadburys.

☐ scientific perspectives, including the source of chocolate, its links to climate and soils and the implications of eating chocolate for heath and diet.

☐ the potential of the topic to reinforce and extend children's subject knowledge of the non European History Study Unit, 'The Aztecs', through links with the history of chocolate.

☐ the language and literacy of chocolate advertisements.

☐ the application of mathematics and industrial and economic understanding, including the making and distribution of profits and the establishment of alternative fair trade companies.

☐ moral and social questions, including the fairness of trading arrangements involving cash crops, the legacy of colonialism in such an international trade and opportunities for international co-operation through the development of initiatives for fair trade.

It is important to note that the students chose this subject because they recognised the relevance of the topic to children's interests and their own; indeed their presentation involved the sharing of a delicious chocolate cake they had made. As well as links with the Aztecs History Study Unit, the students also signalled the potential for linking this work with a geographical study of a distant location where chocolate is produced, thus introducing issues of justice, rights and economics into a geography programme at Key Stage 2.

With respect to 'promotion of democratic processes' they had demonstrated an ability to participate actively in a collaborative task. They were also developing the professional competences relating to 'management of controversial issues'. Although their presentation lacked an analysis of their own positions vis-a-vis the chocolate trade, it did promote a discussion amongst the student audience of the morality of such a trade and of their responsibility as western consumers.

The students' work provided evidence that they were developing those competences identified under the heading 'application of subject knowledge' and that they benefited in particular from being able to draw on each other's subject specialisms. One group commented that they were able to use their knowledge of English to 'examine the chocolate adverts and persuasive language' whilst a history student demonstrated an awareness of interdependence and justice:

> I used my understanding of history to look at how Cortes exploited the Maya and Aztecs — how the cacao bean was brought to Africa and Europe and the history of Cadburys.

The students also extended their own knowledge through researching resources which included a range of materials provided by Cadburys, Christian Aid and Traidcraft products. They commented that they had 'discovered facts not well known to the consumer'.

The students then planned and taught a number of activities to KS 2 children, involving a range of skills and processes. These included making a collage to demonstrate the story of how chocolate went from plant to shop, making a chocolate dessert, and a role-play relating to the distribution of the profits of the chocolate trade. One group designed an advertisement for a fair trade chocolate bar.

Classroom activities: the Fair Trade chocolate bar

What indicators and evidence can tutors look for to determine how far students are developing as global educators? Focusing on one student who worked for over an hour with a group of Year 5/6 children to design an advertisement for a Fair Trade bar allows us to examine how far she was able to develop competences related to the promotion of democratic processes and the management of controversial issues.

She structured the lesson by:

☐ explaining the source of the Fair Trade Chocolate Bar — a local Fair Trading Shop within half a mile of the school;

☐ posing such questions as: *Why do you think children do not buy this bar? How could we make this chocolate bar attractive to buy?*

☐ setting a general task for the group: to design an advertising campaign to make a fair trade chocolate bar attractive to children of their own age;

☐ allocating responsibilities to different children
— to design packaging
— to think of a brand name
— to create a slogan or catch phrase;

☐ inviting children to vote on suggestions where appropriate;

☐ organising the presentation of ideas and the final version of the advertisement to the class;

☐ inviting feedback from the class on the effectiveness of such an advertisement.

These procedures indicate a student working towards many of the competences required of the global teacher. She is aware of the need to introduce children to issues of justice and interdependence and there is indication of increasing competence in the promotion of democratic processes where she uses children's experiences and encourages independent learning. She herself likened the process of her lesson to a design process which included consultation and democratic decision making, comments which indicate that she has made a strong connection with her own subject specialism — design technology — and citizenship education.

Case Study Two
Classroom activities:
mapping the world

The second student, main subject humanities, wanted her class to understand world maps from different perspectives. She had a variety of maps available: among them a Eurocentric Peter's Projection, a Pacifico-centric and a polar-centric. She structured the lesson by:

☐ getting the children to rank the maps in order of most to least familiar;

☐ posing such key questions as:
Would you say these unfamiliar maps were wrong?
Why might these maps have been cut like this?
Who might want a map with Australia in the middle?

☐ showing the children a globe and getting them to draw maps from a variety of perspectives.

Both tutor and student agreed that most of the children responded well to the task. One boy in particular offered many suggestions as to why maps could be constructed differently. The student then analysed her own teaching using the competences above.

> I felt I was OK on 'Controversial issues'. I did offer them the chance to detect viewpoint but it's hard..... I felt I could try a lesson about different viewpoints with maps

because it's about factual things. But thoughts, feelings, emotions — that's harder.

She was making progress towards the competence of 'promotion of democratic processes'. However, using the above criteria helped her realise that she had not been allowing equal access to all children, as the domination of one boy had excluded others from the conversation. Her dilemma was that he had:

> come up with the right answers at the beginning so I wasn't sure what the others felt. They let him dominate the discussion. It was difficult to let the others have a say.

She realised that she would need to be aware of this in future and try to ensure that the other children contributed more equally.

Having the 'facilitation of collaborative groupwork' identified as a competence had helped her, she said, because 'then you know what to aim for'. She felt she had achieved this when the children ranked the maps and drew their own afterwards. She evaluated her 'application of subject matter knowledge' as sound because she had provided a wide range of teaching materials with different perspectives, but added that she was only able to do this because 'I'm a humanities student. I had the background'.

Rather than evaluating her lesson merely at the level of 'it went well', which can happen if there are no clear criteria against which to judge performance, measuring herself against the required competences enabled the student to analyse her teaching so that she could build on her increasing skills and awareness. In the same way, the tutor was able to use the competences to challenge the student's thinking, asking her to reflect on the possibilities offered by map work for looking at neutrality, controversy and the values promoted by an anglocentric perspective.

Conclusion

The significance of such a list of professional competences for use within initial teacher training courses does need consideration. The requirements of DfE Circular 14/93 mean that the focus of the students' taught courses and their school experience is likely to be on those technical competences related to the National Curriculum, and in particular on the planning, assessment, recording and reporting of children's work in the core subjects. Certainly in the immediate future the Ofsted inspection of institutions providing initial teacher training will be mostly concerned with these processes.

Such pressures should not, however, undermine any determination within the profession to continue to promote a reflective approach to teaching and learning which can develop vision, imagination and critical awareness in educating pupils. This is why the production of an alternative list of professional competences as described in this chapter is so timely. We believe that the teachers who will be taking on increasing responsibility for judgements about the professional competence of students will want to promote such an awareness and understanding of the whole curriculum. It is also to be hoped that HEIs will want to ensure that subject application modules include

opportunities for students to explore the contribution of that particular area to the process of educating for citizenship in a changing world. We also hope that these competences for the global teacher will support the students who are already showing concern for wider social and environmental issues.

CHAPTER 6

A Curriculum for Courage

Gillian Klein

As we place new steps of change, we need — amongst many other roles and identities — the Teacher, he or she whose life-work is to shape, to impart and to recreate a curriculum in the nation's schools, colleges and universities. The curriculum in its turn helps to build shared courage and a shared future.
(Robin Richardson: *Fortunes and Fables*, 1996)

Preparing teachers to teach means requiring them to think about essential issues: what they want to teach and why. For the kind of education promoted throughout this book, this will take much courage. The contributors are all agreed on what global education is not: not anglocentric, not eurocentric, not monocultural, not exclusionist, not elitist or hierarchical. Many also insist on the relevance of race and gender. And they are clear about the pervasive nature of global education: it must be manifest not only in curriculum content but in teaching and learning styles, in school ethos and so in school policy and management. To meet this challenge takes even greater courage.

For those of us trying to shift thinking from the narrowly national to the global, the actual educational environment throws up its own obstacles. Can we teach teachers to consider issues of justice in the wide world, to trade exploitation as exposed in *Go Bananas*, say, while ignoring the racial discrimination going on in teacher education? (see, inter alia CRE, 1988; Siraj-Blatchford, 1990, Showunmi and Constantine-Simms, 1995). Can we expect the students themselves to pervade their work in schools with a global perspective while simultaneously disregarding the racial abuse and harassment that may well be evident in classrooms, playground and possibly even staffroom? (see, *inter alia* Macdonald et.al., 1989, Troyna and Hatcher, 1991; Klein, 1993; Channer, 1995; Nehaul, 1996). I believe that global education can never be anything other than antiracist.

This is why courage is called for. Despite the rhetoric of the English and Welsh National Curriculum which all concerned with equality issues have used for our own purpose (see for instance *Equality Assurance in*

Schools, Runnymede Trust, 1993), the underlying purposes of the government shapers of existing educational policies have little to do with equality, antiracism and certainly not with global education. The welcome requirement of education for citizenship, even when broadly interpreted by teachers in the classroom, evidently comes from a very narrow perspective on citizenship. I shall return to this later.

Tim Brighouse and other contributors refer to this narrow vision and I want to tease out the dilemmas that we all face. Since I cannot eliminate the negative, let me at least expose it, as a prelude to accentuating the positive, looking at what might be done and drawing inspiration from what is already being done.

Confronting the negative

As I have observed elsewhere (without attracting any contradiction from the Right itself):

> The battle for (education for) equal rights and social justice has come to be fought out in the political arena. The playing field has been marked out by the Radical Right and does not currently appear to be level. The polarisation of *equality* and *quality* and the notion that each renders the other impossible, is a persistent argument of the Radical Right. With assistance from the tabloid press, this false dichotomy has become an established myth. Equal opportunity has itself been redefined by the Right according to the premise that everyone starts out equal and those who are able and industrious will succeed (Klein, 1994).

This view from the right is not only false: it is immensely damaging. It smacks of the geography textbooks in my 1950s school, which made it clear to us little white South Africans that the reason that our black population was poor was because they were lazy. Yet when I looked around me, all the people labouring in our homes, on the streets and factory floors, all the people who were cooking, cleaning, carrying, digging, building, were black. Their ability and industry got them nowhere.

Few students engaged in becoming teachers are likely to have backgrounds that afford them such experiential knowledge. Indeed, many come directly from school and have grown up in a market-oriented society upheld by an ideology that values self-interest above the social good. Most have grown up in monocultural environments, and, for reasons that we shall explore later, almost all are white.

Nor do these students emerge from, or operate in, an **education system** concerned to foster equality and social justice.

Increasingly over the past fifteen years, the far Right policy makers have driven education. This is reflected in the government appointments to policy-making bodies such as the National Curriculum Council, Schools Examination and Assessment Council, now replaced by the Schools Curriculum and Assessment Authority (SCAA). All are government-appointed quangos representing neither the teaching profession nor the local electorate. All have significant figures drawn from the Centre for Policy Studies, the radical Right think-tank, set up by Margaret Thatcher and Keith

Joseph in 1974. The slow growth of the grant-maintained sector means that another tier of government appointed quangos (Funding Agencies) is steadily replacing democratically elected bodies (LEAs).

In July, 1995 the chief executive of SCAA publicly attacked what he termed the 'prevalent' view that no set of customs or traditions was superior to any other, and came down hard in favour of an exclusionist and elitist model of 'British' culture. Despite the brave battles that have been waged, most significantly in English and History, to broaden the parameters of the **National Curriculum**, Ron Dearing has merely cut down the unmanageable long Orders without changing the tenor of the curriculum. Whether children have teachers who consciously and courageously extend the curriculum from 'national' to global remains a lottery.

Initial Teacher education itself has been revised in direct response to a pamphlet written by the Deputy Director of the Centre for Policy Studies. A new quango, the Teacher Training Agency, now runs all teacher education. With the purse in its hands, the TTA is squeezing the four year degree, narrowing the hours spent in academic centres and shifting the emphasis from pedagogic theory and its relation to classroom practice, to strategies, skills and classroom management. Postgraduate students have proportionally even less time to learn about child development and the social and psychological factors which affect learning, since the TTA defines the hours deemed appropriate for the purpose.

The last of the bad news relates to **ethnic minority teachers**, of whom there are less in schools than ten or twenty years ago. The CRE's report of 1989 still holds true: most are on the basic scale, constantly passed over for promotion, teach in shortage subjects or in Section 11 posts (another highly problematic area), and are often subject to harassment as well as discrimination.

In 1993, the Higher Education Funding Council of England (HEFCE) accepted bids from 17 teacher education institutions for funding discrete projects to train more ethnic minority teachers. Accounts of what happened in these institutions indicate that quite a number were inadequate and that some were even exploitive. The projects that do appear to have been effective have in common certain features that contribute to their success. According to Robbins (1995), these include:

☐ ethnic minority staff already permanently in post

☐ established antiracist policy and practice in the ITE

☐ a commitment to sustain the programme after the one-year funding from HEFCE ended.

This was not, however, the case in the majority of the institutions. Far more widespread was a scenario where a black project leader or researcher was appointed for the one year of external funding — and then put out of work. In *Teachers for the Future*, the black editors, Showunmi and Constantine-Simms, and their contributors reveal part of the more common picture. Certain experiences echoed across the country: for one thing, the project leaders had to explain repeatedly that they were in fact staff, and not one of these black students who had suddenly appeared in the white institution. Many felt that the only support came from the students themselves.

The students, for their part, experienced a good deal of racism. Worst of all appears to have been in accommodation and on school practice. Again there is a chorus of accounts about how, on teaching practice, the student found her or himself to be 'the school's black experience'. Also recurring is the way in which the student was then expected to deal with the racism encountered in the school — the school managers and the TEI were content to see it as the student's problem and offered no support.

Rosy accounts of these projects now adorn the publications lists of established academics in these institutions. One (rejected) submission to a journal gave an upbeat account of a project in which, in reality (though never mentioned in the article) only three of the six students managed to endure the year's course. Meanwhile, the fall-out is immense. Students are left with anger or a sense of having failed, instead of with qualified teacher status. Ethnic minority project coordinators or researchers, turned out after the one-year government funding expired, are now without jobs. What chance of global education when there is so little welcome even for black British and Asian British teachers in their own national education system?

Accentuating the positive

Despite all the political pressures — the teaching profession discredited throughout a decade in the tabloid press, teachers deluged with mountains of NCC documents, each contradicting the last, the years of inadequate and often derisory consultation, and the passing of a swathe of education acts — teachers are still there in the schools, though there are rather less of them, doing their job. Many, moreover, are still imbued with the professional ideals and standards with which they came into teaching (see Richardson, 1996). Battered and exhausted though they may be, teachers have not lost heart. Teachers who were committed to social justice in the more egalitarian 1980s still are; teachers who taught according to development and global education principles still do. Research into education and race still attracts reputable researchers and reasonable funding; European money supports education against racism and xenophobia (see, for instance, Massey, 1995).

In addition, there are books like this one: indeed most major academic publishers feature books on their lists that are about equal opportunities in education, about global, environmental and development education. The World Studies Project has had considerable impact (Fisher and Hicks, 1985; Hicks and Steiner, 1989; Steiner, 1993). The development agencies are reviewing their own approaches and educational publications: there is at last a shift from the incessant focus upon the rural aspect of the developing countries — a focus that is hardly appropriate when already seven of the world's largest cities are in the South and the move to the cities is accelerating far faster than in the North (Grunsell and Wade, 1995).

The expertise and knowledge about global education is increasing, not diminishing. The present book is both a reflection of that knowledge and a contribution to it. Global education has a following in many institutions and schools but it is by no means part of all teachers' practice and as it is not explicitly part of the National Curriculum, is not statutory. It will take both energy and courage to fly against the prevailing wind. In suggesting what we need to do and how, I return to a paradigm institution that I invented for the purpose of a similar argument (Klein, 1994) and contextualise my suggestions within it.

Revisiting Eden

To envisage a model of teacher education that supports global — and therefore antiracist — education, I return to my imaginary paradigm institution. This is how I described it:

> Every aspect of Eden Institute of Education is designed to facilitate equal rights and promote equality of opportunity. Respect and rigour are the touchstones: respect between and among staff and students, rigour in intellectual inquiry and analysis in assessment standards and procedures, are integral. It is a professional body in which ethnic minority representation of both staff and students matches the national percentage, or is higher if the institute serves and draws staff from a region of high ethnic minority settlement. At each level, from academic board to new

appointments, there are similar numbers of women and men. Buildings are designed to ensure that the physically disabled can contribute fully. The ethos reflects and sustains the approach of everyone at Eden: to be purposeful and rigorous in study and supportive to colleagues...

> What Eden provides is twofold: a permeation of equal rights values — *and a global approach* — across the entire overt and covert curriculum , and also discrete units in which all aspects of teaching and learning are studied in relation to issues of race and gender equality, special educational needs — *and a global perspective.* (Klein, 1994 — italicised passages added).

At Eden, I suggested, all students followed an obligatory, albeit brief, course on the social and political factors that can lead to differentiation in education, while also being expected, throughout their training, to consider all areas of the curriculum in terms of both the statutory requirements and of accuracy and a world perspective. They explore how myths, stereotypes and 'common sense' racism and sexism are constructed and the role of the media in legitimating certain views and values. They are encouraged to become critical viewers of television and film, critical readers of newspapers and books, considering always: whose interests does this presentation serve?

Among their assessed work, students give a short presentation of how an event of an international nature or occurring in a developing country was portrayed in the English media. They are required to review a novel written by and offering insights into, a culture and background different from their own, thus encouraging empathic as well as empirical understanding. Acclaimed writers such as Toni Morrison, Wole Soyinka, Amy Tan, Vikram Seth, Anita Desai, Timothy Mo are among many that widen our perspectives on the world.

The Eden curriculum

All subjects are better taught and learned from a global perspective. In respect to the core curriculum all students need, for example, to know the world-wide and particularly Chinese, Indian and Arabic origin of Mathematics (see Ross, 1984) and to be able to show children that all people in all parts of the world use mathematics in their daily lives (see Shan and Bailey, 1991). Similarly in Science, students learn about the chemistry employed by the earliest potters in Africa — almost certainly women! — in baking clay pots; about the inventions of Morgan and McCoy (see Andrews, 1994) as well as Faraday and Marconi and, most importantly if global education is not to be tainted by outdated but not extinct stereotypes, about the fallacy of notions of biological determinism.

Students are required to explore their own curriculum areas to extend their knowledge and perspective: as well as the texts suggested in this paragraph; they will find useful King and Reiss (1993) and Runnymede Trust (1993) pp24-49 and chapters throughout this book.

As well as curriculum content, students at Eden reconceptualise their understanding of the 'curriculum' using the model set out by the African

National Congress in 1993, to assist in the transformation of education in post-apartheid South Africa. It states:

> The curriculum is understood to be more than syllabus documentation. It refers to all the teaching and learning activities that take place in learning institutions. It includes the aims and objectives of the education system as well as the specific goals of learning institutions: what is taught, the underlying values, the selection of content, how it is arranged into subjects, programmes and syllabuses, and what skills and processes are included; the strategies of teaching and learning and the relationships between teachers and learners; the forms of evaluation and assessment used; how the curriculum is serviced and resourced; how the curriculum reflects the needs and interests of those it serves ... (ANC, 1993)

Add to this only that the curriculum should take into account also the future of learners as world citizens in an interdependent world, and Eden provides a model for curriculum development that has global education at its heart. All we need to adopt that model is courage.

CHAPTER 7

Initial Teacher Education and Global Citizenship: the Context of Permeation

Sneh Shah

Introduction

Permeation, a model articulated powerfully in the Swann Report (1985), can be applied to issues of global citizenship in Initial Teacher Education. This will require a focused approach to course development involving students, teachers and teacher educators. Suggestions are made based on practice in gender and race work, taking into account the complex nature of education about global issues in the current educational context and climate.

Developing a context for global citizenship: the permeation model

Education for global citizenship is a broad concept rather than a discrete body of knowledge about the world and thus presents a challenge to teacher educators. In order to become positive citizens, young people at the end of secondary schooling should be capable of making rational decisions and taking appropriate action in the context of a just global society, of which they are members. To help them achieve this their teachers need to be equipped as follows:

☐ have understanding of the issues in global citizenship;

☐ have belief in the relevance of global citizenship for children;

☐ have the ability to select the right teaching content, resources and methods;

☐ appreciate the significance of non-formal education within educational institutions;

☐ have the skills for self-development.

Thus the task of teacher education is to broaden the attitudes of the student teachers so that they understand the meaning and rationale for global citizenship, develop a commitment to a global model of citizenship, have the ability to be reflective and critical and, at the same time, innovative and adaptable. The emphasis is on students' personal development as well as the development of their professional skills, whereby they would pass their commitment and readiness to take action, as appropriate to the children. The fact that it is not obviously a part of the National Curriculum makes it even more vital for teachers to have the conviction and the skills to make global education an integral part of their work.

Thus it makes sense for the total experience of student teachers to be affected by concern for global education, defined as:

> ... a concept of education for democratic citizenship, for local, national and global responsibility which is embedded in human rights and a commitment to social responsibilities (Lynch, 1992).

If we accept Lynch's definition, we accept a focus that goes beyond the mere acquisition of knowledge about global citizenship. The whole process of education undergone by the student teachers and then by the children they teach, should be a democratisation process.

Permeation thus appears to be the answer. The Swann Report (1985) described permeation in the following terms in relation to teacher education and cultural diversity:

> Any course of study is informed and permeated by various assumptions, conscious or unconscious, which condition the selection of subject matter, the approach adopted to it and the emphasis laid upon various parts of it.

Two areas that have to a certain extent successfully permeated 'mainstream' education are multicultural/anti-racist, and gender education. Multicultural education has had a strong take-up in education, in the DES/DFEE, and the LEAs, with some effect on teacher education. This may partly be due to events in the wider society, eg the so-called riots in the early 1980s. Gender has been on the agenda because of the Sex Discrimination Act (1975), the Equal Opportunities Commission, and the economic trends which have accelerated the need to bring more women into education and thence employment. Whereas issues of race, culture and gender are directly linked to wider social consequences. Racism, for example, is seen to exist among children and adults, and it has been established that children's educational achievement has in many cases been negatively affected by it (eg Rampton Report, 1979; Modgil, Verma, Mallick and Modgil, 1986; Commission for Racial Equality, 1987; Gillborn, 1990; Klein, 1993). Lack of global awareness has no such direct social effects, however, so there is no legal or social impetus for global education.

The task for teacher education is immense. It is made even more daunting by the fact that the current position of global citizenship in teacher education is generally insignificant. There may well be a number of reasons for this:

☐ Global education has not featured to any great extent in the National Curriculum. The theme of Citizenship (when cross- curricular themes were an important feature of the National Curriculum), looked at a whole range of issues related to citizenship at home, as opposed to global (NCC 1990). Teaching about global citizenship differs from the teaching of content-based subjects such as mathematics and it is possible that many teachers might not wish to or be able to give the guidance and support student teachers may need. The extent to which school staff are able to keep up with current developments is partly related to school budgets and the priority given to global citizenship. So different schools may afford students very different experiences.

☐ The agencies that create areas for funding/special initiatives, like the Higher Education Funding Council (now replaced for teacher education by the Teacher Training Agency) are not influenced by the global education lobby, although currently more attention is being paid to environmental education.

☐ The work being done by the aid agencies such as Oxfam and Christian Aid *inter alia*, and organisations such as the Council for Education in World Citizenship and the Development Education Association has on the whole touched teacher education only superficially. It has tended to focus on school pupils and teachers and on work with teachers in schools, but not very much on teacher education.

☐ Focuses such as global education are still likely to be categorised as left wing radical politics, as opposed to 'good' education.

This situation has several implications. First, a good case needs to be made to justify global citizenship so there is real, not tokenistic, commitment. As is detailed below, institutions have to adopt the case for global citizenship as an integral part of their policy. Tokenistic policies will in practice mean statements on paper not being implemented, or mere gestures such as providing recycling banks. Secondly, the students entering teacher education courses are likely to be anywhere along the continuum, from the very oppositional to the fully committed. Even when they show some concern, this may spring from low-level media information (eg Comic Relief), which could in some cases have generated/confirmed a hierarchical view of societies/cultures and countries in the world. The conviction may also be related to one aspect of global education, such as care for the world's finite resources, without their having any awareness or understanding of the issues of power relations which cause or contribute to the world's resource problems (eg the debt burden and trans-national economic production).

Educating them, in the sense of informing them about complex global issues, is thus essential.

Permeation of global citizenship: the way forward

Nature of suggested permeation

For the student teachers to gain full understanding of the issues and be able to continue developing, a much broader course is needed. Shah (1989), in relation to gender and race, identified the following areas:

- ☐ Staff development
- ☐ Resources
- ☐ Courses/scheme validation procedures
- ☐ Style of delivery
- ☐ Core (compulsory) and other elements of training
- ☐ Organisation of core (compulsory) element
- ☐ Evaluation by staff and students
- ☐ Follow-up to evaluation and monitoring
- ☐ Institution/department approach to permeation
- ☐ Allocation of responsibility for permeation

Yet one of the problems with permeation, as highlighted by the Anti-Racist Teacher Education Network (1988), was that it could be 'a road to nowhere', when all that happens is no more than paying lip-service. All too often courses have been validated and there have been statements in the course documents to the effect that there will be permeation, but it has not happened in reality. This necessitates a search for a mechanism or strategy that could ensure that institutional/course strategies on permeation are being implemented.

The following main points, made in light of the fact that future students are likely to spend more time in schools than higher education campuses, aim to ensure there is effective permeation, and that the students' development is progressive. Issues such the selection of appropriate resources and teaching methods are not touched on in this chapter but are dealt with elsewhere in the book.

Development of overall institutional policies

Fogelman (1991) describes citizenship as:

> becoming an interesting hybrid: as a dimension it alludes to school ethos, democratic processes and interaction between groups, and becomes an all-pervading whole-school approach, which demands a school management strategy.

This can be applied with equal relevance and importance to the higher education institutions. For permeation of global awareness to be effective, there has to be institutional recognition of its relevance and commitment to implementing it. Institutional policies on global education are virtually non-existent, although some emphasis on environmental education (for instance, the University of Hertfordshire's policy on greening the curriculum), are a sign of the changing times.

The process of developing the policy is important to overcome staff resistance (reflecting the low priority of global awareness in society as a whole) and to create within the institution a genuine understanding of the relevance of global citizenship in the education of the students and the children. Like all policy, it will need to be ongoing, with a structure for evaluation and monitoring, and review.

Developing and monitoring specific courses

There is literature available on the process of developing, evaluating and monitoring courses.(eg Swann Report, 1985; Gundara, Jones and Kimberley, 1986; Myers, 1992; Runnymede Trust, 1993). However, to ensure that this happens across all courses, and that there is understanding of the issues, the academic committees of the institutions can undertake to:

☐ require that the process of developing the course involves the dialogue needed to ensure that promotion of global citizenship as relevant to the course can take place; and

☐ require that in the annual monitoring and evaluation reports, there is adequate analysis of the implementation of the objectives, as stated in the validated course document.

Institutional committee/working party

The implementation of a policy, especially one dealing with what some may regard as controversial issues, needs to be sensitive to and work on student concerns. Within the overall institutional framework, it may be relevant to have a working party related·

to a particular scheme. Staff and students working in partnership, and students taking their share of responsibility, should be demonstrated at the level of planning as well as implementation of courses. For example, the School of Humanities and Education of the University of Hertfordshire has an Initial Teacher Education Equal Opportunities Working Party. This includes students as well as staff, and also practising teachers. Student development also means the staff need to understand where the students 'are at'. Practising teachers are involved because students need to relate their learning at the higher education institution to the reality of schools. Having perspectives from schools can help the staff devise their teaching to provide a basis for a true partnership.

Curriculum content

Students require opportunities to explore wider issues, especially those seen to be controversial, at some stage of the course. This is vital if they are to understand the essence of global citizenship and its value so that they can map out their own development and be in a stronger position to make appropriate applications in their teaching.

The core curriculum content should include examination of:

☐ The complex and varied elements of global citizenship such as development and peace. Just as with terminology in the field of culture and race (multiculturalism, anti-racism, multi-ethnic education), students need to be aware of the different educational responses, (eg peace education, global education) so that they can work out their own meanings and frameworks.

☐ Place and work of the aid agencies. There is widespread belief that images of the world are as shown by the aid agencies (in order to collect funds) and that this is the only work that the agencies do. Students need to be made aware of the way images are created and sustained. One headmaster for example recently told a PGCE student on school experience that he would never use aid agency materials as they are all biased, ie only emphasise the negative aspects such as poverty and disease. This helped the student to begin her own process of critical reflection.

☐ Reports such as Brundtland (1987) and The Report of the South Commission (1990). These would provide a wider context for the students to understand global interdependence.

☐ Up-to-date surveys of children's and young people's views about the world, to counterbalance the belief of certain education psychologists that children should only be taught what they can directly experience.

Linking issues and methods

Permeation runs the danger of being patchy across the different subjects and all aspects of professional studies. The course development document should include a grid that would list the different courses/elements, and indicate which aspects of global citizenship will be implemented at what stage. The grid should list, as appropriate, knowledge, teaching methods, skills, resources. Such a grid should also indicate the nature of progression in the students' learning.

The working out of the grid by course tutors should enable different issues to be brought together as appropriate. For instance, awareness of the nature of stereotyping will be relevant also to issues of racism, culture, gender and disability. Such bringing together would help the students in understanding how issues are interrelated, how they can organise their work (for instance, under topics) and still be able to advance the children's understanding.

There are other advantages in making such links. Most students will have some awareness of multicultural issues, even if at a superficial level. Focusing on letting people (eg minority ethnic people, women and girls) talk about their own experiences will enable the students to appreciate the need to let people in the South speak for themselves, rather than people in the North being, metaphorically speaking, the interpreters.

School-focused work

Opportunities have to be found to utilise the increased time spent by students in schools.

☐ Schools are usually involved in activities outside the curriculum that have the potential for work for global citizenship. Schools may organise fund raising in relation to a tragedy such as an earthquake in India. There may be a particular school theme such as caring for the local environment. Students should, as a part of their education in schools, be expected to focus on such activities and do an analysis of them.

☐ The students can use the opportunities presented in their classroom experiences to explore the children's level of understanding and knowledge in relation to global issues, and build up an understanding of their development of global concepts and images.

☐ The work being done by the children can be the basis on which students work out how to extend the children's understanding, from local to national and global issues.

☐ Assessed assignments can be made very productive. One example is that of the TENET project at Sheffield Hallam University, where gender issues were a part of the assessment of the students' teaching practice (Sheffield Hallam University, 1991). A practical way forward would be to get the students to produce a portfolio which they can develop over their various school experiences. This could include the work being done by the schools and how that can be extended, the nature of children's understanding of the world and implications for the teachers' work, or the production of a catalogue of available resources. This can be an independent study which would to a certain extent overcome the deficiencies in schools' approaches to global citizenship. This can apply to teachers as well as to students, as:

teachers cannot be expected to be experts on all the current issues..Part of their training ....needs to be in how to discover and use what resources are available (Rogers, 1993).

Conclusion

Recent changes in higher education have significant implications for the teaching of an issue such as multicultural, gender, or global citizenship education. In particular, note needs to be taken of the increasing emphasis on shorter courses, larger classes and less staff-student contact time. A teaching approach that focuses on the students' personal development and entails some attitudinal change is likely to be affected by these changes; students need to be tutored through the process so that they are convinced about the educational value of the topics under discussion and are aware of how essential their own continued development is.

However, parallel to these is a new emphasis on more student-centred learning, and students taking greater responsibility for their own learning. There also needs to be a recognition of the changed role of the tutors, from knowledge-givers to facilitators and supporters (Shah, 1994). The result could be that, provided there is commitment within the institutions to furthering global citizenship, students' learning can become wider than a rigid discipline-based curriculum led by the tutors. Students may be able to bring a focus on their learning which could reflect their concerns and ideas about the world.

There will be difficulties in implementing a comprehensive approach on the lines described in this chapter. However, the generally increasing public awareness should mean that the higher education institutions and the Teacher Training Agency will have to respond. In many respects there may be advantages in trying to permeate global citizenship when there are changes in both higher education and in the school structures, as this enables fresh thinking to take place. The words of Andrews (1994) in relation to the National Curriculum, that '...for the globally minded teacher it is neither a gag nor a straitjacket but a challenge', apply equally to the whole current framework for teacher education.

CHAPTER 8

Resources for Global Understanding

Marjorie Drake

The disorder of the world surfaces in school in many ways and the qualities that are needed to address the global crisis are the very same qualities required in school (Lamont et al, 1993).

Introduction

National development and environmental agencies, and others concerned with global issues, have a long tradition — predating the National Curriculum — of producing classroom materials to assist teachers in exploring the wider world in the classroom. A large variety of resources thus exists to help the teachers who want to foster global understanding in primary and secondary schools. These materials are generally reasonably priced, attractive to look at, practical, cross-curricular and designed for the active participation of pupils in their own learning.

However, Global Education is not merely about formal learning in the classroom. While many of these resources address specific areas of the curriculum, they are also concerned with the whole ethos and atmosphere of the school, the nature of the school environment and the behaviour of all who work within it. Thus they provide a double boon to all classroom practitioners — student teachers, NQTs and the experienced. This chapter explores the thinking behind the production of these resources and reports on how a representative sample were used by student teachers.

Why produce resources?

Most of the voluntary, non-governmental organisations (NGOs) who are concerned with world issues produce educational resources — between two and twenty each year per organisation. Sales range from 500 to the best-selling ActionAid photopack locality study, *Chembakolli, a Village in India*, which has sold over 14,000 copies to date. Resources are also produced by Development Education Centres, which in turn are substantially funded by these national NGOs. What are they aiming to achieve by this?

I looked for answers from ActionAid, CAFOD, Christian Aid, Friends of the Earth, Oxfam, Save the Children, UNICEF, World Wide Fund for Nature (WWF) and Birmingham Development Education Centre. In a questionnaire which probed the educational and other thinking behind their publications, education staff ranked a series of statements as well as providing detailed answers to factual questions. The representatives whose responses are quoted are identified by the name of their agency. It is important to note that these quoted views represent the policy of the education departments whose work is part of the wider programme of that NGO.

There was strong agreement among all the agencies questioned that the most important outcome they hoped for was a change in attitudes, so that pupils would develop a realisation of interdependence, would be able to celebrate diversity instead of fearing it, would place a value on all life and be aware of the need to live together and share resources. Other top priorities were: breaking down stereotypes, improving understanding of other cultures, overcoming racism, empowering people to take control of their lives, and increasing understanding of the causes of poverty.

Developing democratic skills (such as communication, co-operation and participation) was also a high priority for half the participants. On the other hand, encouraging lifestyle changes, for instance through questioning consumerism or recycling, was not universally seen as the most important

aim. UNICEF said that this was '*not in the forefront of their aims, as there were other agencies giving these areas a very high profile*'. One of these was WWF UK, who placed this objective at the top of their list.

With one exception, all agreed that their educational resources were not about raising money. UNICEF, which runs a high profile 'non-uniform day' every year to raise funds in schools, says of this event:

> With its substantial education pack and little reference to actual fundraising, (non-uniform day) seeks to reach schools with the values and skills enshrined in your list. I consider that we are in the vanguard of introducing DE (Development Education) to schools where it is previously unknown.

A representative from ActionAid did give fundraising a high priority, but he linked this with raising awareness and increasing understanding of poverty which, he felt, should in turn lead to a change in attitudes and action such as campaigning or fundraising. Certainly none of the agencies see any direct fundraising coming out of their education work:

> Our primary relationship with schools is educational and therefore we do not make general fundraising approaches to schools....We believe that fundraising activities should deepen understanding of the issues behind the need, in a way appropriate to the age and experience of the young people (CAFOD et al, 1990).

Save the Children felt it was important to raise awareness of the gap between North and South in terms of *justice* rather than material wealth. It also gave top priority to the development of critical awareness — a questioning approach and an open mind.

Campaigning for change was the foremost aim for CAFOD and second for Oxfam and ActionAid. However, this came fairly low in general. Most of those questioned gave development rather than environment as their main focus, though there was a general consensus that the two were linked. Only WWF put equal emphasis on both. It was also difficult for people to separate out whether they were most concerned with improving knowledge, skills, or attitudes.

> Can you change your attitudes if you do not have the knowledge and skills to do this? Knowledge is not enough unless it is taken further with changed attitudes and actions,

was Oxfam's comment. Where people did prioritise, most put attitudes first, although ActionAid said knowledge and skills were more important 'because of the curriculum'. These were things that could be assessed and monitored, whereas it was very difficult to prove a change in attitudes! However, for the majority, this was seen as the underlying aim. Save the Children said it was more important to give children experience (of the lives of other children and families) than knowledge.

Birmingham Development Education Centre is one of the largest DEC producers of resources. While agreeing with most of the aims mentioned in the questionnaire, it sees the process of creating the resource as paramount. All its material is produced in collaboration with teachers, so that it is involvement in curriculum development which provides a focus, concentrates the collective mind and furthers the participants' creative development. It becomes an added bonus to share the results of this active, collaborative process by marketing and disseminating the work.

There is an ongoing debate within most of the NGOs about the importance of providing resources for schools, compared with the rest of their work. When funds are short, it can sometimes be seen by some in the agencies as a luxury they cannot afford. Others feel it is more important to try and influence decision makers, particularly those in the countries they work with. So the education lobby has to work hard to make sure its voice is heard.

Listening to the South

It is of crucial importance to listen to the voices and opinions of people from the southern countries of the world, who are often ignored or marginalised but frequently the 'subject' of classroom materials. We asked those who produce the resources in this country which portray people in the South, how far the people were consulted, and who else took part in the preparation of the material. This question related particularly to the locality packs.

Half the agencies said the people portrayed were always consulted, and the others that they consulted occasionally. All collaborated with teachers in this country but only four also sought the views of teachers overseas. Teacher educators in the UK were asked for their opinions by six agencies but only three also asked those overseas. There was always consultation within agencies of their overseas personnel, whether based here or overseas. Others who help with preparation of materials in the UK are DEC workers, and natives of the countries concerned living in this country.

Birmingham DEC, whose materials are developed and produced by local teachers, places a large value on 'well-constructed study tours', where dialogue can take place *in situ*. It also felt that the interests of those who would use the resources needed to be taken into account, and that they should be treated as partners rather than simply as receivers of information.

Attitudes for a fairer world

Clearly the different organisations do have distinct emphases, with UNICEF and Save the Children concentrating predominantly on human/children's rights, CAFOD and Christian Aid on the faith dimension and the idea of justice, Oxfam and ActionAid wanting to raise awareness of poverty while promoting positive images of poor people. While both WWF and FoE place their main focus on care for the earth, they acknowledge that this is closely linked with care for people, and WWF in particular has a strong global awareness.

But although the emphasis may be different, it is clear that the over-riding aim of all those producing resources for use in schools is to influence people's attitudes. All recognise the need to develop a global perspective in pupils *and* teachers, through increased knowledge and understanding of

countries and cultures other than their own, greater environmental awareness, and more understanding of the causes of poverty and injustice leading to respect for others and a desire for a fairer and more sustainable world.

There are many opportunities throughout the primary and secondary curriculum to raise such awareness, and materials have been produced in all subject areas by the agencies surveyed here specifically to address the National Curriculum requirements. Moreover, these resources are based on principles of student-centred, active learning involving group discussions and personal reflection that encourage democratic processes and individual growth.

Resources for developing global teachers

How far do these resources, produced for children and young people, help the teachers who choose to explore these issues? What contribution can they make to the professional development of student teachers? A range of universities and colleges in England and Wales asked their student teachers to use some representative NGO materials in the classroom or, if this wasn't possible, to study them carefully and evaluate them (see Appendix I for list of materials).

The following section, based on evaluations undertaken by students throughout England and given to me by the colleagues who teach them, focuses on students' responses to some exemplar primary resources. It thus provides some indication of how students training for teaching are preparing to become global teachers within the framework of the National Curriculum. Their comments are also refreshing evidence of their professional understanding.

Using photograph packs

Thematic collections
Save the Children's packs *Doorways* and *Homes* explore a similar theme, providing images of contrasting homes world-wide as well as case studies of poor housing and homelessness, and the variety of ways in which it is being tackled. Both packs are aimed at Key Stages 1 and 2.

One student who used *Doorways* with Years 1, 2 and 3 found it stimulated both her and the children:

> Pictures were excellent stimuli — children exceeded my expectations... it helped them think out problems and engage with each other in a way they are not used to doing. Good challenging of stereotypes.

Other student teachers had similar results, including good written work. The photographs helped the children realise that everybody in Africa does not live in mud huts, and, furthermore, that people have specific reasons for building houses the way they do. Although expressing some concern about the complexity of the language at Key Stage 1 in both resources, teachers used them in the infant classroom. An overall judgement was that materials such as *Homes*, with its excellent Teachers' Handbook, are 'very useful for exploring economic understanding, social issues, health and environment and caring for others/citizenship'.

Bananas is another popular topic in Global Education, as they are familar to most children and exemplify unfair trade — those who do most of the work producing bananas being denied most of the benefits of selling them. Two resources on the subject were examined: Oxfam's *Go Bananas*, aimed at Key Stage 2, a pack containing notes, worksheets, photos, a poem and a world map; and Christian Aid's free leaflet for secondary students, *Banana Shake* (see below).

The Oxfam pack was judged by some to be 'a limited but thorough resource' which could be used in science, geography, maths and English. Others commented that its positive images are helpful in questioning stereotypes and that it provides opportunities for the children to work collaboratively, explore the basic concepts of interdependence, similarity and difference, and appreciate the diversity of human experience. The black and white photographs received some negative comment, and this is a factor to consider when producing materials for the ever-proliferating locality study packs.

Locality packs
These are photo and activity packs focusing on a specific part of a country, to comply with Geography requirements. They have widespread appeal and are produced by all the agencies as well as other bodies (e.g. the Geographical Association). Students judged these on the whole to be very good introductions to their subject, with plenty of information made accessible to the children. People liked the photographs and were able to achieve

their aims of comparing and contrasting Britain with a distant locality:

> I used every activity in the pack (*Chembakolli: A village in India*) as I felt each activity helped to progress the children ... they already had their own ideas, however at each stage these misconceptions were reduced... I used the pack to explore multicultural awareness and understanding... the usefulness of the pack was immense.

Several students, however, were aware that to use these packs on their own would give a limited view of the region, and that they would need to be supplemented, as using them in isolation could reinforce rather than break down stereotypes and preconceptions. All found that they would be particularly useful for the geography themes of settlements and environmental change, and for teaching map skills. Most students were quick to realise their cross-curricular approach — the pack *Living and Learning in a Tanzanian Village*, for instance (which one student rated 10/10) would be useful for 'geography, history, RE, English, art, music and technology'.

Books for teachers

Another approach is to produce books which combine an intellectual and pedagogic rationale for the study of global issues along with classroom activities teachers can use throughout the curriculum. The student teachers provided feedback on two such, *A Wealth of Faiths* (Christian Aid, WWF and New Economics Foundation, 1993) and *Learning From Experience* (Steiner, 1993).

The emphases of its three sponsors are reflected in the subject matter of *A Wealth of Faiths*. It aims to show through stories the teachings of different religions about the concept of 'wealth' and how this relates to care for the environment, and is thus useful across the curriculum, but particularly RE, English, economic understanding and environmental education.

Amongst a range of positive comments, an interesting reservation expressed was that the book was biased — 'very green oriented — makes no attempt to give contrary view — treats religion as fact rather than belief'. Nevertheless this student still felt the book to be worth 7/10, and agreed that it provided opportunities for the children to think analytically and appreciate the diversity of human experience. Another who used the book for KS1 children rated it 9/10. It stimulated 'Circle Time' discussions on 'the effects of actions on others', and 'willingness to give up something':

> The children were willing to participate and listen to each other as well as reflect on their own actions. Even the shyest child eventually joined in ...very informative... children enjoyed stories etc... illustrations did not appeal to younger ones.

Learning from Experience is the latest in a series of handbooks from the World Studies Project, following *World Studies 8-13: A Teacher's Handbook* (Fisher and Hicks, 1985) and *Making Global Connections* (Hicks and Steiner, 1989). It aims not only to provide examples of a World Studies approach to the subjects of the National

Curriculum, but also to help with assessment and classroom organisation. It was well received by the students, being rated 'a source of inspiration' and 'a very useful resource book', which gives 'a wider personal understanding of 'global' issues'.

Conclusions

Students judged this representative sampling of resources for Global Education to be a great boon to their present and future teaching, enabling them to 'break down a fairly difficult set of concepts into manageable, understandable, sometimes fun activities and (to produce) a pleasant working environment'. They found information about social and economic issues, in Britain and overseas 'clear and easy to understand... lots of links to the curriculum... many of the discussions can go very deep'.

Many young people training for teaching are committed and idealistic, qualities exemplified in a comment on *Banana Shake*:

> I would rate the pack very highly as it promotes fairer distribution of resources, the respect of human rights...It encourages the individual child to have a whole balanced personality, with a caring sharing attitude. (It) promotes co-operation, questioning, critical analysis, links between rich and poor, justice and keeping commitments.

Global Education is not another subject competing for space in a crowded timetable, but a dimension that can permeate the whole curriculum and ethos of the school. The resources available can help teachers with all subjects of the National Curriculum and in fulfilling OFSTED requirements. But more than that, they will expand their pupils' horizons and contribute to their moral and spiritual development. The student teachers who have used and reflected on these materials are on the way to becoming global teachers.

Let one such student, commenting on her final teaching practice after she had used a range of development education materials, have the last word:

> In my school, many of the children's problems stemmed from the fact that they lived in an inner-city, deprived area. Violence, decay and poverty were all around them. Attitudes to education were rock-bottom. After all, how had it helped Mums, Dads and carers?...

World studies philosophy would argue that schools, teachers and pupils have to look at the causes of these problems, not just on an individual level but also from a local and global perspective, instead of just having to cope with outward symptoms. The problems these children had affected every area of their education as well as their development, therefore to avoid the issues involved is to come across a brick wall again and again as year after year children do not benefit nearly as fully from their formal education as they are capable of doing...

World studies... relates the child's personal development with the external world. It... sets out some ways in which personal, social and moral development and awareness can be achieved. It is the ideals worked through and firmly linked to practice.

Appendix I

Resources examined by the student teachers

ActionAid, (1991) *Development Without Destruction* (game), Chard: ActionAid.

Akhtar, N. and Gyde-Nwadikwa, S. (1993) *Pakistan — Change in the Swat Valley*, Chard: ActionAid.

Ashmore, B. et al (1993) *Mapping Our World*, Oxford: Oxfam.

Brace, S. (1992) *Chembakolli: A Village in India*, Chard: ActionAid.

Brace, S. (1992) *Nairobi: Kenyan City Life*, Chard: ActionAid.

Brace, S. (1992) *Pampagrande: A Peruvian Village*, Chard: ActionAid.

CAFOD et al (1991) *Fala Favela: Shanty Town Life in Brazil*, London: CAFOD et al.

CAFOD et al (1992) *The Great Wave 1492-1992: An alternative history of encounter and resistance in the Caribbean*, London: CAFOD et al.

Christian Aid/ New Economics Foundation/ WWF (1993) *A Wealth of Faiths*, London: Christian Aid/ New Economics Foundation/ WWF.

Davison, S. (ed) (1990) *The Farmer, the Leopard and the Hare*, Chard: ActionAid.

Davison, S. and Gyde, S. (1993) *Just Add Water*, Chard: ActionAid.

Day, H. (1994) *Can Development be Measured?*, Chard: ActionAid.

Day, H. (1993) *How Many Children?*, Chard: ActionAid.

Midwinter, C. et al (1992) *Living and Learning in a Tanzanian Village*, Manchester: Development Education Project.

Greig, S. (1992) *New Faces, New Places: Learning about people on the move*, London: Save the Children.

Grunsell, A. and Stearn, T. (1990) *Go Bananas*, Oxford: Oxfam.

Harrison, D. (1993) *Lima Lives: Children in a Latin American City*, London: Save the Children.

Jarvis, H. (1989) *Clean Water: A Right for All*, London: UNICEF.

Jarvis, H. (1993) *Palm Grove: Study of a Locality at Victoria Falls*, Zambia, London: UNICEF.

Lyle, S. and Jenkins, A. (1991) *A Mountain Child (Peru)*, Carmarthen: Greenlight Publications.

Lamont, G. and Burns, S. (1993) *Initial Guidelines for Values and Visions*, Manchester: Development Education Project.

McFarlane. C. and Osler, A. (eds) (1991) *New Journeys: Learning from Kenya and Tanzania*, Birmingham: Development Education Centre.

Najda, R. and Reid, P. (1991) *Homes: An Active Learning Pack for 6-12 year olds*, London: Scottish DEC and Save the Children.

Taylor, B. (1987) *Doorways*, London: Save the Children with International Year of Shelter for the Homeless.

Steiner, M. (1993) *Learning From Experience: World Studies in the Primary Curriculum*, Stoke on Trent: Trentham Books.

Appendix II: Information

Catalogues and further information on development education may be obtained from:

ActionAid, Hamlyn House, Macdonald Road, Archway, London N19 5PG 0171 281 4101.

CAFOD (Catholic Fund for Overseas Development), Romero Close, Stockwell Road, London SW9 9TY 0171 733 7900.

Christian Aid, PO Box 100, London SE1 7RT 0171 620 4444.

Development Education Association (DEA), Third Floor, 29-31 Cowpere Street, London EC2A 4AP

OXFAM, 274 Banbury Road, Oxford, OX2 7DZ 01865 311311.

Save the Children, Mary Datchelor House, 17 Grove Lane, Camberwell, London SE5 8RD 0171 703 5400.

UNICEF, 55-56 Lincoln's Inn Fields, London, WC2A 3NB 0171 405 5592.

SECTION II
Pedagogies, Partnerships and Practices

CHAPTER 9

Crossing Points and Meeting Places: Geography and Global Perspectives in Initial Teacher Education

Heather Norris Nicholson

Global citizenship, founded on knowledge, skills, values and social action, should be an integral element of education in a rapidly changing world. Events and processes everywhere are constant reminders of the need for curricula which address environmental responsibility, human rights and social justice and other ethical issues.

A world which defies definitions of structured order requires that teachers and learners develop perspectives and skills which explore the contradictions and uncertainties around them. Implementing a reflective and values-based education is harder when other content and priorities constrain curricula and timetables at all levels.

This is not out-dated educational idealism: modern youth protests may differ in form and focus from their predecessors but the search for justice continues. Our students both expect and require their teachers and tutors to address moral and ethical concerns. Schools and teacher education institutions thus cannot function independently of wider shifts in attitudes, ideas and behaviour (Lynch, 1992).

As educators, we need to foster approaches that will help our students to address the complexities of contemporary life. Narrow definitions of space, race, ethnicity and history — by such terms as North-South, East-West, Black-White, First World-Third World — set up false dichotomies, polarise experiences and deny the dynamics of change (Featherstone, 1990). Enabling students to perceive alternative ways of seeing is the bed-rock of personal and professional development on which teacher education must build (IRR, 1994; Osler, 1994).

Curriculum overload tends to marginalise contemporary social and educational issues into abstract concerns or exclude them altogether (Meighan and Harber, 1989). But it is not just time or resources which limit educational vision: externally-imposed criteria mean that staff and students also face increasingly specific political objectives which may be incompatible with professional obligations and educational beliefs (Menter, 1992). As a result, uncritical assumptions may remain at the expense of mature reflection upon students' prior experience and informal learning (Taylor, 1986, 1987; Tomlinson, 1990).

Global citizenship and cultural pluralism present specific challenges when working with students in predominantly monocultural settings. This discussion focuses attention upon three inter-related themes: how to replace the well-meant but sometimes rather woolly — even contradictory — liberalism among current students with more critical responses to issues of rights and responsibilities; how to foster intercultural dialogue through linking curriculum issues with subject specialist courses and also, how to build upon informal learning.

In this chapter student learning is first related to experiences in particular settings. Three case studies then illustrate specific issues which have arisen when working with student teachers developing curriculum and specialist interests in geography. The final section summarises some of the professional, practical and moral implications for teacher education.

Contexts for student learning

Many formal and informal ways of learning influence how people question and reflect upon the worlds of experience around them. Basic characters of institutional life affect students' search for understanding. Geographical location, recruitment trends and historical connections, mission statements and projected images, subject combinations and the balance between teaching and research influence students' experiences and their perceptions of the social landscape of Britain and the wider world.

In areas with a predominantly white British population, it remains possible for student teachers to have relatively little formal contact with people from other ethnic and cultural backgrounds (Menter and Braunholtz, 1990). They, like the population in general, tend to over-simplify the diversity of both visible and the so-called invisible minorities. Groups are 'othered' with disregard to the historical and geographical contexts of their presence and participation within society. People are linked regardless of race, ethnicity, religion, gender, generation, education, language, status and place of origin. Student awareness of ethnic minority experience derives from hazy awareness of problem and policy response unrelated to the dynamics of race, culture and social change.

Encouragement of philosophies and practices which are responsive to pluralistic communities and world concerns has particular relevance in monocultural settings (Roberts et al, 1994). Well-meaning liberalism can sustain unacknowledged forms of racism and global parochiality;

damaging distortion and confusion arise from naive misunderstanding as readily as in more overtly hostile contexts. Critical use of commercial, community and self-created resources, as well as outside speakers and placements, visits and exchanges, become key means by which staff endeavour to broaden students' experiences and foster more informed professional awareness of global and societal relations.

For monocultural student groups, excursions to contrasting localities are often central in raising global issues and multicultural awareness. Frequently such visits involve going to urban areas with distinctive patterns of ethnic concentration. Realistically, students may meet an alternative monoculturalism rather than gain a true immersion in cultural diversity. Fears of being intrusive outsiders sometimes reinforce student hesitancy and sensitivity: their professional alertness to new situations is tinged by unfamiliarity and uncertainty about the goldfish-bowl syndrome in which they find themselves. On such occasions, the practical difficulties of absorbing students into schools as observers rather than helpers also combine with limited time to lessen the potential for meaningful dialogue.

Important as school visits may be, their limitations require that there are other means of alerting students to the multiple and changing identities of communities in Britain and elsewhere. Monocultural student groups need to become more familiar with the socio-economic, cultural and historical dimensions of minority experiences and perspectives. Closer links between subject specialisms and curriculum studies may offer important foundations for pedagogical development.

For instance, a module on migration, settlement and community available to students in education, geography and other subjects explores how Britain has become a multi-faith, multi-lingual and multicultural society. Processes of racism, exclusion and discrimination set community and school-related issues in context. Many education students select topics relevant to their professional understanding — urban experience, language needs, employment trends, law and order, immigration, travelling communities and identity — and set important educational issues within wider debate.

Ideally, as students question their own positionality — their sense of self and place within society in relation to others — preconceptions and assumptions also come under scrutiny (Epstein, 1993, Roberts et al, 1994). Being British has many meanings both in and beyond Britain. Centuries of socio-cultural and political processes have produced *frames of reference* which construct and impose contemporary notions of identity and belonging (Modood, 1992). Recognising what shapes how we respond to both familiar and less familiar worlds is a prerequisite for the global teacher.

Closer links between student experience and theoretical awareness develop professional judgement and practical skills (Epstein, 1993). Classroom competence cannot be a surrogate for intellectual activity. Informal learning also plays an important although under-emphasised role in developing students' global awareness, particularly in monocultural situations. Contemporary living is, by its very nature, part of a global system upon which students should reflect since neither they nor their future pupils function isolated from outside influences (Bovey, 1991).

Working with others

Student encounters with professionals of Black, Asian or other non-European origin (Grosvenor, 1990) are restricted by deeply embedded discriminatory processes which limit both employment opportunities and entry from overseas (Solomos, 1995). Yet direct contact and familiarity is crucial in sensitising students to how processes perpetuate ignorance, bias and distortion of both historical and contemporary experience.

Only by breaking through stereotypes can students consider how and why identities are imposed, adopted, reproduced or rejected. All too frequently, the replacement of one name-tag for another excludes people from being understood on their own terms, as individuals and representatives of a particular place, time and combination of ideas, beliefs and values.

The curriculum must address the *ethnicity paradox* (Richardson, in Modood, 1992). An understanding of ethnic difference and shared experience involves accepting why people assert and value their own past, language and traditions to both define and defend themselves within a changing world. Cultural understanding comes not from head-long confrontations but by meeting a range of people who can communicate effectively about what it means to be *somebody* doing what they

do and making sense of the world in a particular way.

Case study I: Hearing voices

Southern Voices, an organisation based in Manchester, has a mandate to further cross-cultural understanding through providing access to non-European perspectives. Providing speakers is one strategy amongst a number to bring together people from widely different backgrounds to share insights, information and experience.

A half-day workshop led by a visiting Kenyan academic introduced first year students to links between theatre and development. Through story-telling and more formal presentation, students learned how colonial and post-colonialism affected educational freedom and denied people the right to express themselves in theatre, language and other cultural forms. They discovered how imposed laws and cultural values may perpetuate forms of racial intolerance and injustice under both past European colonialism and current Kenyan governmental policy towards their own cultural and ethnic minorities (Mumma, 1993).

Seemingly distant material had compelling immediacy: colonial steps to replace traditional drama with imported amateur theatricals and the banning of religious performance as witchcraft exemplified eurocentric arrogance and the clash of cultural values. Decisions which could deny minorities their environmental as well as cultural freedom likewise provoked debate of democratic values and ethical rights.

Both examples reveal the official condonation of injustice. They show

how power operates through repression, law and coercion and structures social relations (Rabinow, 1984). Students saw how ideology can reify, disparage and seek to impose identities. Such issues transcend the specifics of time and place: the effects of legislative change on travelling communities in Britain added a comparative and topical dimension on government response to the accommodation of difference.

These issues inform ways of thinking about race and racism and make explicit the inadequacy of narrowly defined national identities. No single voice can represent the diversity of any society. An understanding of how a nation defines itself involves individual subjectivity as well as a sense of belonging to a wider whole. As Gates writes, in an American but no less relevant context:

> We value solidarity, but we chafe under it, struggling to establish individual subjectivity (Gates, 1994).

This workshop revealed the inadmissibility of trying to sum up the so-called South, or Third World or a Developing Nation in a single representative voice. Unwittingly, the southern voice name tag became as erroneous as other labels — a denial of humanity's complexity and contradictory nature everywhere.

Case study II: Shared space, divided space

This section examines some of the complexities surrounding intercultural collaboration. Ten overseas post-graduates worked with a group of geography and education students on a module which explored how different societies value and care for their historical properties and landscapes in times of peace and war. Through working with these mid-career professionals, the undergraduates compared attitudes towards conservation, planning and history in European, Middle Eastern, Mediterranean, African and Asian countries.

Case-studies ranged from Belfast to the Balkans, from Beirut to Baghdad and included the 'heritage conservation' of such diverse sites as York, war-damaged European cities and slave trading stations in Ghana. The course linked academic study with actual events and daily news. Students examined values, democracy and social justice in a global environment.

Professional awareness grew as issues linked to development education, global studies, human rights and citizenship. At one level, the work became a politicised focus upon a specific kind of people-environment relations: it had much potential for prospective primary geography specialists alert to environmental educational approaches. At times it also seemed that these encounters brought new awareness about humanity itself — people's sheer capacity to suffer and to impose suffering but also the will to survive.

Afterwards, all participants acknowledged the merits of having set up this opportunity for intercultural dialogue. Different perspectives and new audiences proved stimulating for everyone. This collaborative work also highlighted the need to plan and run such sessions with great sensitivity.

Each educational community encompasses a unique and specific ethos reflecting the shared experiences and individual styles of its members. Visitors may transgress these unwritten codes unless alerted to them. Informing visitors about what students in general expect need not negate the individuality of their teaching style but may avoid misunderstanding and mismatch.

Other perspectives inevitably reveal differences as well as shared interests. Certain divisions may occur between the visitor and the student group: varying expectations about gender, age or formality, and a visitor's teaching experience or awareness of audience needs require forethought. A speaker's oral competence and confidence or even students' familiarity with hearing English spoken with other accents may affect the success of a visit.

Such common sense practicalities assume particular significance in intercultural dialogue. A positive student learning situation readily provides models for classroom practice. The capacity for misunderstanding is considerable and stereotyping can work in both directions. When a presentation is under-prepared or content is pitched too low, students may sense that they, their course and even their institution are not fairly valued. Likewise, provocative statements and confrontational tactics may inadvertently polarise relations rather than foster better understanding. Such responses reveal how both process and content need careful planning if the potential benefits of such intercultural encounters are to realised.

Case study III: A message from elsewhere

Student teachers respond readily to comparative study of human rights, social relations and environmental citizenship. A module on the settlement, society and landscape of Canada introduces aspects of culture, environment and sustainability in another highly industrialised and urbanised country. Teaching relies upon visiting speakers, audio-visual materials and a range of texts from government, private sector, commercial and voluntary agencies.

Deep-rooted conflicts over Canadian identity, environmental responsibility and national unity invite comparisons with Europe and elsewhere. Relations between Canada's First Nations — the original inhabitants or indigenous peoples — and dominant society require students to unravel cultural, political and environmental complexities and provoke questions about equity, environmentalism and democratic citizenship in an era of global capitalism.

Fur-trapping and hunting provide a provocative entry point into discussing traditional lifestyles within a modern context. Heated debate arises when students try to reconcile opposing views on cultural rights and animal welfare. To the student opinion 'Live and let live' the implicit riders are 'wherever possible' and 'within acceptable levels of sustainable management'. Their responses demonstrate student realism and their own awareness of social vulnerability when external processes undermine a community's economic survival and *raison d'être. A distant issue has relevance to their own lives.*

Understanding indigenous people within modern society involves seeing beyond the constructions of colonial guilt and romantic myth: personal testimonies convey past experiences, present circumstances and future goals. Creative writing from published and unpublished sources speaks directly to students on cognitive and affective levels.

Wanted: someone who cares (see below) comes from a school committed to culturally sensitive curriculum development for indigenous students. The school places much emphasis upon realising personal potential and helps its students to develop both traditional and contemporary skills and outlook.

The poem captures a young person's search for self-identity and realisation.

Its message is familiar to many undergraduates involved in their own search for individuality and has prompted much questioning of ethnicity, national identity and cultural expression in such a heterogeneous society as Canada.

As minorities struggle to redefine themselves and their place in societies everywhere, seemingly remote concerns may illuminate the experiences of others. Introducing students to Canadian aboriginal issues is riddled with problems of appropriation of voice, misrepresentation and generalisation, to name but some. Bringing together drama and geography students linked a number of issues on one occasion and demonstrates the merits of cross-disciplinary approaches

WANTED: SOMEONE WHO CARES

Who cares enough to accept me as I am,
Who does not condemn me for my shortcomings,
Who helps me to learn from my mistakes.

Who cares enough to respect me as an individual
with the right to learn and grow at my own pace,
and in my own unique fashion.

Who will stand by to help when I need it,
but will release me from my own guilt,
and help me find constructive ways to deal with reality.

Who will encourage me to explore the world around me,
Who will open my eyes and my ears to music,
Who will listen to my questions and help me to find answers.

Who cares enough to help me achieve my full potential,
and who has faith in my ability
to develop into a worthwhile person.
Could this someone be me?

Poem by Shawna Lyn Danielle Panipekeesik (16 years old — Sakimay Reserve), Plains Indian Cultural Survival School, Calgary, Alberta.

to some of the moral, ethical and philosophical aspects of intercultural borrowing and understanding.

There remains an urgent need to use teaching materials in culturally sensitive ways, when tourism, the media, and the global character of high-street shopping encourages dipping into cultural difference and tradition with increasing ease. Global citizenship must not legitimise educational safaris into other realms of experience and belief regardless of the risks involved.

Despite current students' ostensible inertia in political matters, many remain staunch advocates of the oppressed and marginalised: cultural integrity, civil liberties, environmental rights and social justice are discussed and written about with fervour. Teaching should strengthen that commitment by creating cultural encounters — even vicariously — which go beyond one-dimensional representations: acceptance must also acknowledge the differences, contradictions and conflicting value systems. Students realise that global citizenship requires gritty realism about the actuality of people's past and modern lives, not timeless fantasies about social, racial and environmental harmony.

Some reflections

All students need to be able to deconstruct their own cultural baggage of inherited knowledge, especially student teachers, if they are to help pupils encounter a rapidly changing world. Yet I fear that without timetabled opportunities for critical thinking and independent reflection, these recognised elements of degree-level study will gradually diminish.

Working with students in monocultural settings requires striking a balance between helping them to recognise unchallenged perceptions and inherited assumptions whilst also valuing their own identity and experience. Likewise, encouraging students to allow for individual subjectivity as well as affinity and shared experience as they listen to others, must not preclude their own independent informed thinking.

Through such approaches, students readily recognise how terms of reference such as North/South, East/West, First World/Third World and Black/White polarise, simplify and freeze actuality into unrepresentative form. Enabling them to construct alternative notions of ethnicity, understand the shaping of geographical space and processes of historical change is not the prerogative of any single discipline: all subject specialisms have a mandate to assist prospective teachers to an understanding of cultural pluralism and global awareness.

I believe that students have a right to question *how* as well as *what* they learn. Indeed, a paying student body should be able to voice its demands about content, methods and resources in a system which stresses consumer rather than citizen rights. Encouraging undergraduates to explore contemporary issues should be accompanied by adequate support. Student-centred learning must not become a cost-saving exercise in devolving responsibility and reducing resources.

Democratic and interactive teaching and learning styles encourage greater student involvement in course design, delivery and evaluation. They are compatible with the wish to provide student opportunities which are prerequisite for globally-aware practice in schools. Indeed, such trends must not disappear under higher staff:student ratios, imposed time rationing and other changes led by non-pedagogical concerns. Moreover, as current reforms affect teacher education, both specialist subject knowledge and curriculum theory also lie in danger of losing their place in a slimmed-down degree. They too are key agents in helping students to understand cultural plurality and global processes.

A commitment to global citizenship represents a belief in education's capacity to understand the human condition and to challenge environmental inertia, social injustice, inequality and intolerance. None of these concerns should be additions to increasingly disparate degree programmes: rather they are facets of one fundamental and recurring question for all educators — **why** *do we teach* **what** *we teach?* When our work involves education students, the question gains further nuances: **Why** *do they want to learn* **what** *we want to teach and* **how** *will what we teach contribute to their own teaching?*

Global citizenship has the capacity to ensure that newly qualified teachers are ready to engage with worlds beyond as well as within the classroom. I believe its remit extends beyond curriculum content and pedagogical style: decisions and policies on all areas of school development, school-community relations, educational resourcing, financial management and site planning, as well as partnerships, staffing and governor representation are part of wider processes.

A teacher education which does not develop rounded professionals, attuned to the world they inhabit and the needs of their future pupils is out of touch. A curriculum which can respond to change should be at the heart of education: it is not just a damage-limitation exercise in enabling people to understand themselves and society: it also a right from which others may spring.

Acknowledgements

I would like to thank Dr Oppia Mumma, Department of Drama, University of Nairobi and Jaya Graves, at The Southern Voices Project, 300 Oxford Road, Manchester M13 9NS for their help. Much is owed also to Doreen Spence, Administrator of the Plains Indians Cultural Survival School, Calgary, Alberta, Canada for her inspiration and commitment to the protection of fundamental freedoms for Aboriginal peoples. I owe much to past and present colleagues and students for their patience and willingness to share enthusiasm and beliefs.

CHAPTER 10

Learning to Listen, Beginning to Understand: the Skills of Philosophical Inquiry

Chris Rowley and Nigel Toye

Introduction — A philosophical approach to global education

Global education draws its values and issues from the related fields of development education, futures education, education for sustainability, environmental education, and peace education. Each has a distinct perspective, and it can be argued that a global teacher is motivated to communicate a favourite world view drawn from one, or a combination, of these perspectives. They share a commitment to investigate serious, and frequently controversial, issues through the context of the curriculum and a preference for active learning methods.

Despite these common features, each branch of global education is based upon an ethical viewpoint which may conflict with the others. Development

education for example, rests upon a utilitarian ethic in which equality of access to resources is paramount. The contrasting tendency in environmental education is to look to the natural environment itself as the basis for ethical behaviour, eg recycling or conservation are drawn from ecological systems. Such differing ethical standpoints can point to contradictory courses of action and can be problematic as guides for any particular pedagogy.

We contend that problems arise because many practices in global education treat ethics as a set of rules based 'on the nature of human nature' or on the 'nature of nature' itself. We believe that the issues important to global educators are far too complex to be dealt with in this way and that the methods of philosophical inquiry, in which our fallibility is recognised, offer an approach which is more likely to facilitate long term and internalised understanding of the issues raised by global education.

The purposes of this chapter are therefore:

☐ to put the case for further consideration of a pedagogy of philosophical inquiry in the field of global education;

☐ to explore the nature of philosophical inquiry; and

☐ to consider how philosophical inquiry can contribute to initial teacher education.

We have drawn on the work of Matthew Lipman and Ann Sharp (Lipman, Sharp and Oscanyan, 1980; Lipman, 1988, 1991) as the basis for our investigations, adapting their materials as necessary. Their programme is being used extensively in countries as widespread as Argentina, Australia, Brazil, Mexico, Nigeria and Zimbabwe.

Philosophical inquiry in the classroom

The process of philosophical inquiry as used in the Philosophy for Children programme can be summarised as:

☐ Reading texts in the form of stories about fictional children who discover how to reason more effectively and how to apply their reasoning to life situations.

☐ Generating a range of questions and then selecting one to serve as focus in discussing the story. This enables children to encounter and examine many problematic issues.

☐ Being part of the group's deliberations. This helps individuals internalise the process and to become more reflective and begin to think for themselves.

☐ These classroom deliberations begin to evoke thinking that is both skilful and deliberate. It is thinking that uses relevant criteria, is self-correcting, and is sensitive to context. It is not just any kind of thinking, it is critical thinking.

Although philosophical inquiry is suitable for adults and children alike, it cannot be readily employed in the classroom without training. 'Philosophy for Children' is truly cross-curricular, sharpening children's judgement in many subjects while improving their linguistic, logical and cognitive competences.

For the purposes of this paper we have identified two key elements of the process of philosophical inquiry which have particular significance to the global teacher.

☐ the development of a 'community of inquiry' in the classroom;

☐ the importance of the notion of *fallibility* as a key element of thinking critically about our global responsibilities.

Global education has always espoused the principles of democracy, but there is a tendency for particular issues to be pre-selected and the expected outcomes to be anticipated. Diamond ranking exercises, for example, are designed to produce a consensus conclusion. Yet arriving at a consensus is only one aspect of democracy and needs to be preceded by a much broader exploration of the underlying issues through democratic inquiry. Exercises involving decision-making and problem-solving are end points of a more substantial process of learning the skills of dialogue.

The democratic principles behind the notion of a 'community of inquiry' are fully compatible with those underpinning Values Education work:

> The Community of Inquiry is characterised by dialogue that is fashioned collaboratively out of the reasoned contribution of all participants (Sharp,1990).

On the other hand, it must also be seen as a pedagogical process that differs in many respects from the processes of critical thinking as commonly understood by global educators. Steiner (1993), for example, suggests tackling values issues with pupils through techniques such as diamond ranking, sorting strategies and the use of Venn diagrams. The philosophical approach to critical thinking outlined in this paper might use such strategies to support the inquiry, but only in the context of issues identified by the participants themselves, rather than those preselected by the teacher. A teacher trained in philosophical questioning will focus these pupil-selected issues appropriately.

The second of the key elements — that of recognising our fallibility through a programme of critical thinking — is perhaps more contentious. If being a global teacher means preparing children for a world very different from the present one, then, we would argue, we must learn to accept that not only might we be wrong, but that our answers are at best temporary. There are very few pedagogical models in which fallibility in this sense is a central tenet. Even in the growing literature of 'critical thinking' (Baron and Sternberg, 1987; Coles and Robinson, 1989; Fisher, 1990; Paul, 1991) it is difficult to identify a clear and unequivocal commitment to fallibility.

The 'Philosophy for Children' programme

One of the purposes of this chapter is to consider what makes the programme developed at Montclair State University, New Jersey, by Matthew Lipman and Ann Sharp, amongst others, particularly useful for preparing student teachers and pupils to contribute to a world of change.

There are several challenges connected with the introduction of philosophical inquiry into schools.

☐ Developing a real democracy in the classroom:

> *Real democracy* is a fundamental aspect of this programme. It involves a change in the relationship between teacher (or student teacher) and pupil, in which the teacher is required to develop different skills in leading and facilitating group dialogue.

☐ Finding methods of tackling *values issues* in a creative and caring way:

> Philosophy for children involves *caring thinking* (care for the thoughts of other members of the group) alongside the now standard critical and creative thinking.

> We believe that it is this element which makes the programme

particularly appropriate for global education. Global educators have always shown concern to develop group discussion but have tended to choose debate rather than a questioning dialogue.

☐ Finding non-threatening *contexts* through which to tackle issues:

Contexts are provided by the use of fictional stories which enable pupils to distance themselves temporarily from potentially threatening personal issues. The story approach offers an opportunity to challenge the *status quo* and promote social change.

☐ Linking issues such as sustainability and equality to a *sound pedagogy*:

We believe that the approaches to classrooms and learning of Dewey, Bruner and Vygotsky, whose theories are fundamental to philosophy for children, also provide a pedagogy compatible with the key aims of global education.

☐ Encouraging a way of thinking which can be transferred into *sound and appropriate actions* in the future:

For example, the most successful school grounds development schemes are invariably those which have involved considerable initial investment in inquiry. Even planting a tree is never *self-evidently* the right thing to do. We believe that philosophical inquiry offers the most viable route to a society in which action arises from reasoned analysis by a community.

'Philosophy for children' in action

We now look at the nature of philosophical inquiry and ask if these processes respond to this need to develop truly reflective dialogue in the classroom.

Establishing a community of inquiry

The community of inquiry is designed to train participants in how to listen productively and to hear what they are being offered. It provides the opportunity for a dialogue in which the logical, rational, aesthetic, ethical, social and political considerations of a subject are illuminated. Pupils learn to object to weak reasoning, to build upon strong reasoning, to engage collaboratively in self-correction, and to take pride in the accomplishments of the group as well as those of the individual.

They can assess the group's progress towards becoming critical, creative and caring thinkers through shared criteria, asking questions such as *Do we give good reasons and examples and cite criteria? Do we recognise distinctions and connections? Do we seek clarification? Are we sensitive to context? Do we care for every member of the community?*

Introducing philosophical content

The curriculum of 'Philosophy for Children' builds on Dewey's contention that narrative is superior to an expository teaching mode (Dewey, 1963).

This approach taps into children's desire to wring meanings out of stories. The Lipman model uses a fundamentally different approach to most current work on the use of story (eg Birmingham DEC, 1991, 1994; Baddeley and Eddershaw, 1994). Whilst sharing some common features with others, the 'Philosophy for Children' approaches are distinctive in the way in which the participants raise the questions about the story which interest them.

Working with a fiction as the basis for your thinking allows the combination of the cognitive and the affective. Instead of the expository style of text that is most often used to transmit *knowledge*, the learner is faced with narrative and dialogue. 'Exposition is sobering, narrative is intoxicating' (Lipman, 1991). Enticed into the world of the story, the student becomes involved with the ideas embodied in the narrative. The ideas and characters provide a context for the participants to operate within:

> Literature does more than provide us with worlds to dwell in. It

---

Criteria for a fully developed community of enquiry

According to Lipman and Sharp's thinking, the pupil or student teacher:

- ☐ accepts corrections by peers willingly
- ☐ is able to listen to others attentively
- ☐ is able to revise views in the light of reason from others
- ☐ is able to take the ideas of others seriously
- ☐ is able to build upon the ideas of others
- ☐ is able to develop their own ideas without fear of rebuff or humiliation
- ☐ is open to new ideas
- ☐ shows concern for the rights of others to express their views
- ☐ is capable of detecting underlying assumptions
- ☐ shows concern for consistency when arguing a point of view
- ☐ asks relevant questions
- ☐ verbalises relationships between ends and means
- ☐ shows respect for persons in the community
- ☐ shows sensitivity for context when discussing moral conduct
- ☐ asks for reasons from one's peers
- ☐ discusses issues with impartiality
- ☐ asks for criteria

---

suggests to us other ways of living in and thinking about the world we inhabit — ways that might be at odds with propriety and common sense (Lipman, 1988).

Paradoxically, the inherently distancing effect of fiction permits the involvement of the participants while also protecting them from too much self-exposure. The focus is on a world that is *like* the real one but not actually *it*. The pupils can discuss challenging issues and their implications through the surrogates of the fiction. It is as if they are talking *of* themselves and their own beliefs but not *about* themselves. Fiction allows contextual learning with security.

The use of drama techniques, especially role-play, enhances this further. By adopting roles from the narrative, the community of enquiry leader enables pupils to engage even more closely with its ideas, for example through dialogue with someone who, in role, is acting unjustly or requiring help. Thus in 'Where the Forest Meets the Sea' (Baker 1988), the children can respond to different perspectives about environmental change as they interrogate the teacher-in-role. It is the context of the story which is so crucial to the exploration of major environmental issues. The very complexity of global issues requires that learners themselves identify and select the specific concerns they want to explore. What is made paramount is their own ability to communicate their understandings and to make judgements. Drama offers two kinds of community of inquiry; *in-role* dialogue related to the fiction and *out-of-role* reflection on the wider issues.

The importance of philosophical inquiry in initial teacher education

It is a fundamental precept of philosophical inquiry that a pedagogy based on philosophical skills overcomes the desire to promote any particular world view (apart from a democratic one). We will argue that the pedagogy of philosophical inquiry has much to offer initial teacher education and describe the links with global education.

Traditional competences — subject knowledge, control and communication skills, understanding of children and the ability to teach — raise some key questions about the nature of knowledge and the purposes for skills. In Paulo Freire's definition: '...to be an act of knowing, learning demands among teachers and students a relationship of authentic dialogue' (Freire, 1990).

To engage constructively in philosophical dialogue requires training in thinking. This is particularly important to student teachers. Until their personal skills in thinking have been appropriately developed, they cannot teach them effectively to children. Lipman, whose programme is based on Socratic dialogue, suggests that institutions of teacher training:

> ...might have placed the fostering of dialogue and reflective thinking rather than learning and classroom management at the centre of the preparation of teachers (Lipman, 1991).

In our view, these two dimensions should be of at least equal status, since using the skills of 'authentic dialogue' with children enables student teachers to develop insights about teaching and learning with important implications for classroom management.

A number of further questions about initial teacher education arise, which we believe philosophical inquiry can help us to tackle:

☐ are our student teachers able to look critically at their work in subject areas?

☐ How well do they formulate appropriate questions to challenge their own assumptions, particularly in establishing aims and objectives for school-based work?

☐ Can they ask the right sorts of questions to help evaluate a session?

☐ Can they handle complex concepts with children in a way which is self-correcting and responsive to the ideas which children bring to the classroom?

A key challenge of this approach is helping teachers to accept the need to raise the status of the pupil's own ideas and to put their own lower on the agenda. The teacher is fallible and must be able to accept the democratic nature of the community of inquiry, ie learning to listen and to understand others, being prepared to acknowledge one's own fallibility without losing confidence and developing one's own thinking as a result.

Recent classroom experiences

We and our students have been involved in 'Philosophy for Children' classroom work for some time. A 9 year old who had been participating in a once weekly programme for 18 months, commented of the Community of Inquiry:

> ...you have a chance to put your ideas with other people's and then it builds up and then it comes to something totally different. And then you start talking about that and you put all your ideas together and then it's turned into another thing (quoted in Timson, 1995).

Commenting on normal school work, this child stated:

> Mr. Toye, he spends quite a bit of his time with us and tries to understand us: and he asks questions and, I think, if we had more school time doing philosophy, talking to each other about it and talking to the teachers about how we found things out, or writing them down, then that would be better — but we're like kind of rushing through our topics.

The 9 year old had this to say about pupils' ideas and the status of their language:

> Sometimes I think children have a different language to adults and adults have a different language to children, because sometimes they don't understand. When they don't understand they just think we're talking a lot of rubbish, so they just leave us.

In 1994, a group of seventeen students — thirteen Year 3 BA(QTS) and 4 Year 1 BA(QTS) — in the University Department of Education and Teaching Studies at Lancaster, chose to take part in an optional philosophy for children programme. This required committing themselves to twenty extra hours on their timetable and to applying the ideas during their school-based work. One student gave a striking reason: '*to enable children not to worry about being wrong and not to be afraid of not knowing the answer*'. Early responses recorded after half the philosophy course and one teaching practice showed that the students were becoming more aware of how to extend children's thinking and develop listening skills.

While using the programme once a week for five weeks with pupils in Key Stage 1, a first year student teacher began to perceive the need for this new relationship and the challenge of changing:

> I found it difficult just to be a facilitator with young children. There was a great temptation to lead the discussion and tell the children what to think. This was as much because it was expected as anything else. The group of eight Year One children I worked with were not used to being responsible for their own thoughts in class — they were used to being told by the teacher what was right and wrong. They found it difficult to think in terms of different rather than right and wrong (Nattrass, 1994).

At present, training programmes do little directly to help students to develop their own thinking skills. The results of this omission are evident, not only in school-based situations but also in the students' own concept formation. If we aim to produce reflective teachers, we must train their thinking in order to strengthen their skills. This will also develop an acceptance of fallibility which could contribute to more confident teachers.

Using the philosophical inquiry approach can help. Learning to think about the 'big questions' that are raised by philosophical discussion can train the mind to think logically, listen to alternatives, reason, challenge assumptions and make good judgements. As Lipman asserts:

> Because Philosophy is the discipline that best prepares us to think in terms of other disciplines, it must be assigned a central role in the early (as well as the late) stages of the educational process (Lipman, 1988).

One student teacher highlighted certain areas where she saw infant children's skills developing. In one example, her group (ages 5 and 6) were defining what a dog is and had listed some criteria. She noted:

> I pointed out that Rata (the little girl in the story *Hemi's Pet*, [De Hamel, 1985]) had all the qualities they had defined for the dog, except for the tail... We went on to discuss how Rata was different. In this way the children were extending their original thinking. I was helping them look at classification and criteria, to be reflective and critical in their thinking.

Very importantly, she recognised the great need for children to learn to listen: 'I did spend a good deal of time and energy encouraging them to make appropriate connections, to listen and make comments or ask relevant questions'. Crucially, she began to interpret her role as helping the children to: 'become more thoughtful, reflective, more considerate and more reasonable individuals'. Another important development for her was recognising how much the children themselves have to offer and that they are fully capable of philosophic thought. The teacher must be sensitive to this and sharp enough to exploit it.

Reflecting on the way the community of inquiry works, she stressed the need to train for group skills.

> A group has a collective responsibility to the community of inquiry. The facilitator can help make things clearer and provide a focus, but cannot make it work if the group doesn't cooperate... Being part of a group and practising as a facilitator is the only way to learn. It can't be learnt from books because it's an interactive skill — it's different every time the group meets, people are in different moods...

Such processes have considerable significance in the development of understanding where global and environmental issues form the content. This will be more successful when the accent is on two-way communication about the issues involved.

For this student, the school-based work seems to have been essentially enlightening, illuminating the nature of learning. The students' perceptions and experiences have encouraged us to pursue the programme.

The global teacher and the curriculum

The early stages of the Philosophy for Children programme highlight the skills of classifying, making distinctions, asking questions, giving good reasons and recognising relationships. Such skills apply equally to many of the issues identified in global education. There are opportunities to engage with these throughout the curriculum, in statutory subject areas, in RE and in the cross-curricular themes. At every stage teachers and children will be involved in exploring these very contestable concepts which the Lipman programme places at the centre of learning. 'What is a good citizen?' and 'What is humanity's relationship to the environment? ' are not only key questions posed by global education, they are also regularly reflected upon in philosophical inquiry (Rowe, 1994).

Concluding thoughts

We cannot ignore the evidence about the lack of training in critical, creative and caring thinking in our schools and in society. However, we cannot expect a philosophical approach to be imposed. It is a programme which must grow out of a recognised need for radical educational progress.

The Community of Inquiry based on philosophic methods is not just another new idea. The Greeks tackled the *True*, the *Beautiful* and the *Good* and Dewey spoke of *Loving, Caring and Valuing*. The Community of Inquiry embodies all that education should, in our opinion, stand for. It is:

☐   about values

☐   about identifying what we think ought to be

☐ about both the cognitive and the affective.

It is active thinking at its very best and should be at the pedagogic heart of all global education. Our work with both student teachers and pupils has revealed very encouraging responses to the approaches outlined in this chapter. If this interest can be harnessed, we have the potential to create a future generation of young teachers able to develop in children the ability to see the world of the 21st century for themselves, rather than to have it presented with only one, often dated, vision. Global Education is concerned with raising questions yet often it raises instant answers too, answers which fail to involve children properly in dialogue. Learning through Philosophy is a truly active pedagogy which enables student teachers, and ultimately children, to experience this process for themselves, and to begin a journey of discovery, searching and acting upon the questions they ask.

Further information can be obtained from the authors, at the Department of Teacher Education, Charlotte Mason College, University of Lancaster, Ambleside, Cumbria, LA22 9BB
or :
SAPERE
Roger Sutcliffe, The Society For the Advancement of Philosophical Enquiry and Reflection in Education, Stammerham North, Christ's Hospital, Horsham, Surrey, RH13 7NF.
Fax : 01403 255283;
E Mail: 100421.440 @ CompuServe.com
Centre For Practical Philosophy
Department of Philosophy, University College of South Wales, Swansea
Centre For Thinking Skills
Robert Fisher, West London Institute, 300 St. Margaret's Road, Twickenham, TW1 1PT. Fax: 081 8910487

CHAPTER 11

A More Rounded Education: Global Perspectives in Modern Languages and Initial Teacher Education

Kim Brown and Margot Brown

Introduction

This chapter describes our recent investigation into cross-curricular approaches to Modern Language teaching and learning. Margot Brown is National Co-ordinator, Centre for Global Education, University College of Ripon and York St. John, and Kim Brown was formerly Lecturer in Modern Languages Education, University of York, and is currently project co-leader with the Centre for Global Education, York and part-time teacher of French in Cambridgeshire. For the past two years we have been working together to develop cross-curricular activities for the secondary modern language classroom.

The purpose of our research was to try to establish how much experience Modern Language student teachers had

of collaborative planning and teaching with colleagues in other curriculum areas, both in schools and higher education institutions. We wanted to discover to what extent they understood the potential offered for learning about other communities and cultures in the world, through studying a language. This, in turn, can lead them to explore issues of common concern such as equality and environmental responsibilities. Pupils meet these ideas in subject areas across the curriculum — how far did student teachers of Modern Languages understand their responsibility to share the broad educational purpose of preparing pupils for their roles as future citizens?

It is clear that pressure on teachers in their separate National Curriculum subject areas has meant that the non-statutory cross-curricular themes are under threat (Radnor, 1994; Siraj-Blatchford, 1995). Teacher educators need to make sure that new teachers entering the profession have a clear understanding of the importance and the potential of cross-curricular learning and teaching if it is not to disappear completely. Our research started from an interpretation of 'cross-curricular' in its broadest, global sense, to embrace active learning about world issues. We share with Byram the belief that learning a language and about the culture of the communities in which the language is spoken are interdependent and that it also involves learning about real issues of the wider world:

> It will be necessary to point out again and again that language learning necessarily involves learning culture and that neither is subordinate to the other. It will also be necessary to demonstrate that the value of foreign language learning as a part of young people's secondary education lies not in narrowly and exclusively preparing them for some future foreign travel but in giving them experience and knowledge in the present which contributes to their understanding and enjoyment of themselves and the world around them (Byram, 1991).

Definitions

In the summer of 1994 we sent questionnaires to one hundred and eighty Modern Language student teachers in six university departments of education in England, with the aim of eliciting their understanding of the term 'cross-curricular' and exploring how much experience they had of teaching and learning in other curriculum areas, both from their university course and from their time in school. Eighty were completed and returned. There were eight questions, seven of which were open-ended and one which involved answers on a spectrum from 'strongly agree' to 'disagree' (see Appendix I). We defined the term 'cross- curricular' in the questionnaire:

☐ in the sense defined by the National Curriculum Council ie themes, dimensions and skills (NCC, 1990);

☐ in terms of collaborative planning and teaching between departments, where resources and methodology might be shared by teachers;

☐ where the aim is to raise awareness of cross-curricular issues of world concern in the target language.

By taking our definition of 'cross-curricular' beyond the themes, dimensions and skills of the NCC to include real issues of common concern in the world, we are suggesting that languages have a central role to play in the educational process of the young person overall. By raising awareness of world issues in school, teachers are helping pupils to make sense of the world and to prepare them for the part they will play as responsible future citizens. Such issues go beyond separate subject areas and involve knowledge, skills and understanding that pupils acquire in different areas of the curriculum. They are in essence cross-curricular. We wanted to explore the perceptions that the student teachers had of their role as teachers of

Modern Languages, particularly in relation to incorporating a global perspective in their teaching and to try to establish the extent to which their courses prepared them for this role in school.

Student teachers' responses: collaborative teaching

Have you had any experience of Modern Languages lessons in which basic resources have been shared between another department and Modern Languages?

Student teachers' responses reflected the range of their experience and the different levels of their expectations of meeting cross-curricular approaches during their training. A common comment was that there was 'not much general collaboration of this sort — faculties seem to keep themselves to themselves with respect to work and there's a lot of jealousy between faculties'. Some students had started to build links with other departments in terms of exchange of resources:

With my Year 7, I introduced capitals ... because I knew they did countries and their capitals in geography. I borrowed equipment from the Science department for 'height and weight'. I did a bar chart/survey of favourite subjects — Year 9 — as I knew they had just done them in Maths.

Students referred to skills such as number work and map-reading, drama and cookery which are common to different curriculum areas and some thought that links between English and Modern Languages would be important because of a shared concern with grammar:

I think links with 'English language lessons' are particularly essential in cohesive grammar programmes. I think pupils would see the usefulness of language if it was used across the whole curriculum

English — grammar so learners understand the function of different parts of speech

English — grammar especially, reading for pleasure.

Those without experience of collaborative teaching said that they 'would like to see more sharing and collaboration within departments and between departments'.

If students have some experience of collaborative work between departments, their understanding of the nature and purpose of this way of working is still very tentative.

Student teachers' responses: the global perspective

Have you had any experience of Modern Language lessons for which planning has been informed by a concern to raise issues with a global perspective which are not specific to Modern Languages eg environmental issues, human rights, equality issues, development education, world studies?

The National Curriculum Areas of Experience offer modern language teachers the opportunity to introduce a global perspective in language learning activities; however, students clearly found it difficult to see the potential of this approach.

Their responses were limited to situations in France and sometimes in Europe in general (there was not one reference to the world context of the languages being taught), to topic areas such as careers, business studies, technology and science (famous French inventors) and to a focus on language structures, for example, one student notes that she used a video on pollution 'to practise the perfect tense'. What we are suggesting in our definition of cross-curricular approaches is that the issue is the starting point and that activities that engage pupils will generate language learning. Through this process, pupils are learning about themselves and the world, leading to what one student called 'a more rounded education'.

Where student teachers do give examples of activities that they identify as 'global', they generally feel that this approach is only possible at Sixth Form level:

> A lot of the topics mentioned above are topics which you cover with the Sixth Form as topics in themselves. Have taught environmental issues, equality issues, human rights under theme of racism.

Several important points come out of this. Students refer to the requirements of the A level syllabus and to the added maturity of the pupils (in terms of both their understanding of the issues and their language competence) as reasons for leaving the teaching of world issues until the end of the pupils' school career. And yet pupils are meeting real issues of world concern in other curriculum areas from an early stage in their schooling and through every level.

In modern foreign languages the National Curriculum Areas of Experience hold the potential for the exploration of global issues at KS3. It is a cause for concern, however, that GCSE does not also recognise the importance of learning about the culture of those communities where the target language is spoken.

Lack of confidence

Where students express their willingness to engage with world issues at A level, with comments such as: 'More likely with older pupils (Years 10, 11, 12, 13) when they have the language to discuss those issues with a better awareness of them', they voice concern about doing the same at KS3, feeling themselves insufficiently informed to make the material meaningful to their classes. It was noticeable from the questionnaire that students felt the need for support from other curriculum areas or from a visiting expert if they were going to deal with world issues such as equality issues and human rights. They found their lack of confidence in their own knowledge about geography a constraint. Teachers and student teachers of modern languages need to be helped to understand that where the emphasis is on learner not teacher, where open-ended activities are set up which allow pupils to bring their own knowledge and understanding from other curriculum areas into Modern Languages, learning is effective and cross-curricular in essence and not wholly dependent on the knowledge of the teacher.

Lack of resources

It may be that when students talk about their lack of self-confidence they are in fact identifying a need for strategies and resources to help them address these issues with younger age groups. There may also be an important area of confusion for modern language specialists here, namely, that 'doing' racism or human rights, for example, means limiting activities to discussion. If pupils do not have the necessary language skills to take part in a discussion then language teachers will not be prepared to tackle this kind of activity. However, there are ways of looking at world issues, of understanding differences and similarities between communities and ways of building up self-confidence, care, and concern for others which do not centre on unstructured discussion and which actively engage the pupils with the issues. There *are* strategies and resources which can support active learning in modern languages before sixth form, some of which are described below.

Teachers working with global education materials and approaches have developed structured activities which can be adapted for use in modern language classrooms at KS3 and 4 (eg, inter alia, Fisher and Hicks, 1985; Pike and Selby, 1988; Baines, 1992; Steiner, 1993; Brown et al [in preparation]. See also Resources listed in other chapters in this book). From our experience, we recommend that more collaborative teaching and planning across curriculum areas is necessary in ITE itself so that modern language students are made aware of resources and methodology in different subjects which can support language learning (see Brown and Brown, in preparation).

Constraints or opportunities?

To summarise, from the students' responses, the key factors which emerge as constraints to adopting a global approach in the Modern Language classroom are teaching in the target language, the student teachers' own lack of confidence to take on wider issues and the lack of resources to support a cross-curricular approach in Modern Languages. While acknowledging the challenges, we want to show that what the students perceive as constraints can be converted into real opportunities to enrich language teaching and learning at secondary level.

Use of target language

The National Curriculum requires that wherever possible language lessons should be conducted in the target language. For the teacher, this means that classroom management, instructions for activities, explanation of grammar points, discipline, socialising and feedback on work should all be done in the language being studied. Pupils are encouraged to interact with the teacher and with their peers in the target language at all times. There are several factors which determine the extent to which this is possible, for example the age of the pupils, their confidence with the language, their co-operation and the continuity and consistency of approach of teachers within a department. There is no doubt that the requirement to teach in the target language can feel like a constraint. It can reinforce pupils' dependency on the teacher for the

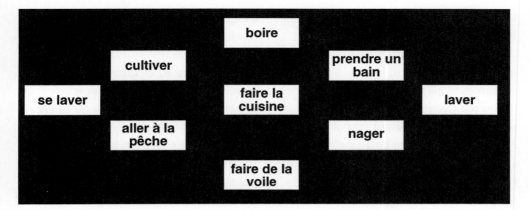

language they need and limit the contexts for learning offered to pupils. However, if teaching in the target language prevents language teachers from offering pupils at KS3 and 4 challenging and effective activities and from engaging with the whole person then we have to look for positive ways round the problem.

Active learning

Structured activities developed in global education can be used to address challenging issues in the target language while giving support at different levels of language competence. In Figure 1 above we provide an example of a diamond ranking activity which formed part of a series of activities to raise awareness of the importance of water in the world. Working in groups, pupils collaborate and negotiate to reach an agreement about their priorities. This activity engages the pupil's knowledge and understanding from different areas of the curriculum and from her experience outside school.

There are challenges. Pupils may feel high levels of frustration because they are very involved in the activity and at the same time limited by having to communicate in the target language. The activity can be supported by word and sentence cards (see Figure 2 below) which offer pupils a range of views to identify with and choose from.

The teacher might take a fairly active role in prompting and supporting pupils' comments in the target language as she monitors the activity. The challenge here is that the language learning is closely linked to the process of the activity: the pupils are learning personal skills in active group work and they are doing all this through the target language. In other words their learning goes beyond learning the vocabulary and language structures.

Collaborative teaching and learning

An activity like this brings Modern Languages close to Humanities. There are many resources such as photo-packs and active group tasks produced by development education agencies which can be used in modern language lessons to support teaching and learning about world issues (see exemplar list in Chapter 8). Student teachers need to be made aware of the resources available and shown how and why they might use them. For example, in a recent school-based mentoring session on cross-curricular teaching, with a group of ITE students from four different curriculum areas — English, History, Modern Languages and Science, we discovered that none of them had met a diamond ranking activity before in their own schooling, on their ITE course or on school experience. If we want to encourage pupil-centred approaches to learning and collaboration across curriculum areas, we must make sure that student teachers are also given the opportunity to explore active learning and to understand the wider educational purposes which underpin them.

It is also important to understand the value of planning and teaching with colleagues in other departments. Not only is there the possibility that teachers might overlap and repeat activities in different curriculum areas but, more seriously, they may offer fragments of knowledge about the world which are never brought together for the pupils in school. Thus if pupils learn French, for example, in their language lessons but do not learn that French is spoken in a number of African countries, and if the same pupils learn about these African states in their Humanities lessons but are not told that French is the official language, then it is difficult to see how they can begin to make sense of the world.

Recommendations

The research described in this chapter is exploratory and needs further work both with future generations of student teachers and with teacher mentors and tutors in university departments of education. Nevertheless, on the basis of this investigation we feel able to assert that there are key areas which need to be addressed to enable modern language teachers to play a full part in the whole educational process of young people.

☐ PGCE courses need to offer a model of collaborative planning and teaching both between university department of education tutors and teacher mentors in school, and between teachers in school in different curriculum areas. This will ensure that I TE students in modern languages understand the part that language learning has to play in the overall learning of the child.

☐ Mentoring partnerships between schools and higher education need to encourage dialogue and INSET about cross-curricular approaches, active learning and global issues in Modern Languages. This will meet the different learning needs of both student teachers and pupils and enhance motivation and involvement in language learning. Such INSET would also be of great value to all practising language teachers.

☐ Initial teacher educators need to be aware of the potential that strategies and resources used in other curriculum areas have to enhance language learning, where pupils are actively engaged in the exploration of real issues which concern them and which help to prepare them for their role as responsible future citizens.

☐ Publishers need to be encouraged to produce language learning materials to complement course books. These can support the National Curriculum Areas of Experience and emphasise issues of common concern using the process of active learning.

☐ Pressure needs to be put on GCSE examining boards to recognise the importance of the cultural context in language learning. The topics and settings at GCSE have the potential to reflect the cultural diversity of the world in which pupils live. The examination needs to give recognition and value to this dimension of language learning.

Conclusion

From this small piece of research we detect that ITE for modern languages may not be effectively addressing the world context of language learning. In the new climate of partnership between university departments of education and mentor-led programmes in school, the opportunities for reflection and practice are there. Student teachers need both personal and professional development if they are to address world issues in modern language lessons effectively. They need to be offered the chance to extend their knowledge and understanding of the world context of the languages they are teaching and of the whole curriculum within which they will be working. Further research needs to be undertaken to establish the extent to which global perspectives are being explored in modern language teacher education and to reaffirm the central role that modern language teachers have to play in a young person's learning in school.

Appendix

Cross-curricular Modern Languages Project Questionnaire

The authors conducted a research study into cross-curricular teaching in all its various forms in Modern Languages. The following is a list of the questions used in the research questionnaire. The full questionnaire is available from the authors c/o Centre for Global Education, University College of Ripon and York St John, Lord Mayor's Walk, York, YO3 7EX.

1. How many lessons roughly have you observed in curriculum areas other than Modern Languages during your course?

    Please give details.

2. From your observations of lessons in other curriculum areas, what kind of links, if any, do you think could be established with Modern Languages?

    Please give details.

3. Have you had experience of any of the following aspects of cross-curricular teaching on your course?

    a. Those themes defined by the National Curriculum Council ie Economic Awareness and Industrial Understanding, Careers Education and Guidance, Health Education, Education for Citizenship, Environmental Education.

        Please give details.

    b. Modern Language lessons in which basic resources have been shared between another department and Modern Languages e.g. maps of the Francophone world from the Geography department, photographs from the History department.

        Please give details.

    c. Modern Language lessons in which resources, information and strategies have been planned collaboratively with members from other departments.

        Please give details.

    d. Modern Language lessons for which planning has been informed by a concern to raise issues with a global perspective which are not specific to Modern Languages e.g. environmental issues, human rights, equality issues, development education, world studies.

        Please give details.

    e. Please indicate if none of the above.

        Have you any comments?

4. Have you tried teaching as described in d. above? [Y/N]

5. Would you be interested in trying it? [Y/N]

6. If yes to either of these, what kind of support would be necessary to make your teaching effective?

    Please give details.

7. The following constraints have been identified by other student teachers. Which would apply to you?

Constraints	Strongly agree	Agree	Disagree
Pressure of increased workload			
Demands of the textbook			
Target language			
Lack of time			
Lack of resources			
Lack of cooperation with other departments			
Departmental policy			
Limitations of personal knowledge			
Not sufficiently convinced of the need			

Other constraints:

Please specify

8. Have you any further comments?

Please specify

CHAPTER 12

Re-enchanting the World: Education for Change in the 1990s

David Hicks and Kay Wood

This chapter gives an account of the development of a new course at Bath College of Higher Education, called International Education and Change (IEC). In particular it describes the introductory module, called Education for Change (IE101), and how the first students responded to it.

International Education and Change

The subject

International Education and Change asks questions about the sort of education needed in Britain and Europe to meet the demands of the twenty-first century. What challenges will have to be faced, what role will education play in society, and how far will education in its present form be able to meet the global needs of the next century?

The modules for this subject are located along three dimensions. The first is cultural and geographical. Modules investigate examples of conflict, communality and change that exist in the European, English and Welsh education systems. By focusing on current issues, the subject matter provides a dynamic medium through which an understanding may be gained of the structure and organisation of education in Europe.

The second dimension is a values dimension. It is impossible to study the previous modules without having a critical awareness of underlying ideological stances, but this dimension focuses specifically on notions of education for equality, justice and human rights on scales from the local to the global. It looks at education as a force for change and as an aid towards creating a more sustainable future. The third dimension contains modules which give a vocational focus to the subject by allowing students to gain applied educational and training skills in particular fields.

Even though higher education is changing, the stress on strong subject content and a clear definition of what constitutes 'academic knowledge' remains. Yet this very demarcation affords little space or opportunity for either staff or students to consider the crucial global changes of the day (Orr, 1992). Education Studies, for example, has never quite enjoyed the academic status that more traditional subjects have. This proved to be a bonus in the creation of IEC, since it allowed for unlikely connections, interesting juxtapositions and 'new' knowledge. It also gave an opportunity to extend experiential learning strategies which tend to have played a small part in traditional higher education courses.

The tutors writing the modules came from a variety of backgrounds in education, the humanities and social sciences. Most had been involved in teacher education. In this context there has been growing concern with the failure of current Education Studies to provide little more than a reactive stance to recent government initiatives. Tutors recognised the potential for change and in IEC seek to present education in an international and global context. The word 'change' is included in the title as a reminder of the importance of this concept at all levels of education and in society. The world is in rapid change, the dominant educational paradigm needs to change, staff and students need to change. A new spirit is abroad as the new millennium approaches.

The institution

Bath College of Higher Education is an independent institution accredited to validate its own courses and offering a range of degree programmes in the fields of education, humanities, human ecology and the creative arts. These are taught through a largely modularised system which has allowed staff to diversify and students on different programmes to avail themselves of a number of pathway options for their qualifications. IEC partly arose out of the need for staff diversification in the Faculty of Education with the increasing move of initial teacher education into schools.

The students on IEC come from a variety of backgrounds. Several are school leavers but an increasing number are mature students, many of whom have come to college through Access routes. Most will be studying for a BA (Hons) Combined Award. This regular clientele is augmented by students from other European countries on ERASMUS programmes. IEC students thus come from a variety of cultural backgrounds, many widely travelled and having substantial life experience. They range in age from eighteen to fifty and many are on programmes that contain a teacher education component.

In 1994-95 the forty students on IE101 were from the UK, the Netherlands, Belgium, Germany and Portugal. In particular IEC has a core of Dutch and English students who are studying for a joint International Degree awarded by Bath College of Higher Education and the Hogeschool Rotterdam. Initially the Dutch students found the switch from one education system to another quite difficult because they were used to a very full timetable and rather formal teaching. Having to be responsible for managing their own time at college and being expected to think creatively and independently was a new experience for them.

Education for change

The introductory module

What should the first module of this new course encompass, we wondered? What would most give a flavour of the educational needs of the twenty-first century? After much deliberation we agreed that there should be a two-fold emphasis on contemporary educational issues and on global issues. The outline programme for the first semester is shown overleaf. The timetable allowed three hours contact time per week, in the form of one lecture and a longer seminar. We agreed that the seminars should model the experiential and participatory modes of learning that are at the heart of good global education.

Our choice of global issues was dictated partly by a desire to use the 1992 Earth Summit as one of our benchmarks and partly by the time available. The first half of IE101 was thus an introduction to the state of the planet, with particular emphasis on environmental issues, development issues, and the nature of a more sustainable society. The second half of the module looked at some of the main educational responses to such issues during the 1980s and 90s, viz. global education, environmental education, education for equality and futures education. We tried throughout to emphasise a range of differing ideological responses to these concerns.

Amongst the recommended texts for the course were *Daring to be a Teacher* (Richardson, 1990), *The Earthscan Action Handbook for People and Planet* (Litvinoff, 1990) and *Educating for the Future* (Hicks, 1994).

Student responses

How did students respond to the teaching of this module? When asked at the end of the semester what they valued most, many highlighted the mixed nature of the group and the opportunities this afforded to meet and learn about different cultures. For Inga, it was the assortment of nationalities:

> I really like that in this course there is a mixture of different nationalities, so that we can listen to a variety of opinions and possible solutions for ecological/global/ gender problems.

Jill, although not herself straight from school, welcomed the chance to meet and talk with students older than she was, whom she felt she had much to learn from:

> It's good to hear from others, in particular the mature students who have a great deal to offer.

In evaluating the course, students highlighted both the topics explored and the learning process itself as being important in what they had enjoyed or gained from their studies. There was little of the gloom sometimes associated with courses on global issues, although one mature student felt that the knowledge he had gained had made him more pessimistic:

> A raised awareness of the issues lead me to read more and that gave

Education and Change: Outline Programme

1. **Where are we now?**
    An introduction to each other and the course, and to some global issues and educational experiences

2. **State of the world**
    Key issues raised at the Earth Summit and the Cairo Population Conference, some arguments and debates

3. **Changing paradigms**
    Contrasting different value positions on the current global crisis and contemporary social change

4. **Environmental issues**
    The nature and origins of environmental problems today, green philosophy and perspectives on action and change

5. **Development issues**
    The nature and origins of underdevelopment today and the growing gap between rich North and poor South

6. **Ecofeminist perspectives**
    Differing feminist perspectives on contemporary society and the particular contribution of ecofeminism

7. **A sustainable society**
    Definitions of, debates about, and examples of more sustainable ways of living

8. **Education and ideology**
    Differing perspectives, value positions and therefore priorities, in relation to education and training

9. **Vanguard education**
    A socially critical approach to education and examples of innovative curriculum developments in the UK

10. **Environmental education**
    Education for sustainability and the difference between education about, through, and for the environment

11. **Education for equality**
    Issues of inequality and equality in society and in education: dilemmas, insights and propositions

12. **Futures education**
    The need for a more explicit futures dimension within education and the development of futures thinking

me a deeper sense of pessimism but also a desire to try to do something about the state of the world (Stephen).

A central tenet of the course is that students should be aware of current issues of global concern and also of the possibilities for personal, social and political change. In this way it is hoped that IE101 will not leave students feeling disempowered. Several of their statements indicate that they see plenty of opportunities for creating change. Sometimes they felt that they had changed at a personal level because they now had more knowledge or because, in one case, the course as a whole had rendered them almost breathless. Asked to draw a picture that symbolised the module, Claire drew her face, hair on end, mouth wide open, astounded by what she had learnt and experienced! Jane highlighted the environmental knowledge she had gained from her study of acid rain:

> I learnt about acid rain, the seriousness of the damage we've done. I wouldn't have been aware without writing this essay, learning about how much damage we're doing generally. It is never talked about, people ignore it.

Knowledge inevitably leads to changes of opinion and to an awareness that attitudes generally need to alter. Yasemin recognised this need to change and thought how this might be translated into action.

> It might help me in my future because now I'm aware that we all have to change our behaviour and our attitudes towards the

environment and I've got an idea of what could be done to achieve sustainability.

Many of these students are aspiring teachers. In their evaluations, almost all emphasised both the need for educational change and the realisation of the impact that they could have on future generations:

> I understood that there could be a better alternative, that there are options that can be worked to and goals to achieve (Jean).

> I feel this module may help me to educate children who hopefully I will teach in the future so that they will inherit a world and be aware of the mistakes that previous generations made and make good (Peter).

Petra summed it up well when she described how personal change would lead to specific changes in her work as a teacher in Germany.

> I am more sensitised now although I was informed before. I'm now more aware and have special ideas on how to integrate these topics in primary school education.

All the programme themes (opposite) struck a chord with some students, but four were of universal interest. These were ecofeminism, changing paradigms, development issues and a sustainable society. The areas of the course most valued appear to be those which held the imagination, offered some vision of a different way of doing things or showed that people's worldviews are open to change.

Learning about ecofeminist perspectives was of major interest and cited again and again by both women and men (Diamond and Orenstein, 1990). Melissa, for example, felt that this enabled her to make links with the past as well as to look to the future:

> Ecofeminism interested me most, looking back to ancient civilisations and realising that women were once more equal and realising how this had changed.

In particular we looked at Milbrath's (1989) work on changing worldviews or paradigms and the notion that a shift is occurring from the Dominant Social Paradigm to a New Environmental Paradigm and the idea that we live and work within an overriding cultural paradigm that structures our lives but which is open to change.

> I enjoyed the word 'paradigm'. I had never heard it before (Max).

> I am interested in changing paradigms, ecofeminism, (using) timelines. All these issues have added to the limited knowledge I had (Isabelle).

As well as the content of the course, students were interested in the learning process itself. We specifically emphasised the value of experiential and participatory learning and these activities all worked well. The most memorable activity for the group was Blind Trust. They worked in pairs, taking it in turns to be blindfolded. The person that could see took their partner on a walk round the campus to explore the environment in as many ways as possible. Deprived of sight, the students became acutely aware of their other senses. We also used a role-play game about conflicting interests in Amazonia. They remembered:

> The one when we went outside and pretended to be blind - I learnt a lot about trust that day (Lucy).

> Placing ourselves in the shoes of different ethnic groups who are driven out of their surroundings (Gladys).

> The live activities... served to draw my mind to the course (Remco).

Finally, the students demonstrated in their evaluations that they were more aware of the political dimension of social change.

> I learnt about the distribution of wealth. I know more about issues which I had no knowledge of before. It's frightening that important information is not known by most people in the western world (Susana).

> I found that education in Britain is...decided by the most powerful (Jane).

Staff responses

Kay's reflections

I came to this course from a long background in teacher education and a growing disenchantment with current trends. Students in initial teacher education appeared increasingly to be skilled technicians rather than reflexive practitioners. Moreover, the most urgent issues of the day seemed to be totally overlooked. I sensed a growing need for change in myself, felt excited but also nervous about the direction this change might take. I still felt disconcerted when students like Jill said:

We don't usually talk about these things in higher education. These are the things we talk about with our friends over coffee.

What did this mean, I wondered? Was she saying that this wasn't real knowledge, not the stuff that academic degrees are made of? Or was she saying that at last we were touching the concerns of the students. I hoped it was the latter. Sabien seemed to confirm this:

> For me the seminars are not only on Tuesdays from nine till eleven but also during the rest of the week. I really want to do here and now something about the points we discussed in the course.

The experience of teaching IE101 has resulted in a steep learning curve for me and I am conscious not only of increasing my knowledge but also of a number of unintended outcomes which the seminars afforded. The students often surprised me by the connections they made.

The exact relationship between education and issues to do with the state of the world still remains problematic for me. Was the module about issues to do with education or global issues? How do the two really relate? In choosing to separate them the way we did (see the programme), we seemed to have relegated education to a second-half appearance only. In retrospect, I think that we need to enmesh them more securely next time round.

Perhaps not surprisingly, things that had moved me also seized the students' imagination. I am pleased with the apparent success of this first teaching of Education for Change and the many levels at which the students engaged with the subject. I am also delighted to find that the European students felt themselves to be integrated into the course to the extent that Remco could write:

> It is good to see how much consideration you took of the presence of foreigners.

Dave's reflections

For me preparing and teaching this module was like a huge breath of fresh air, after the mechanistic National Curriculum restrictions of the last several years. Having been pushed to the margins of the curriculum, the state of the planet and global education could now come back centre stage where they necessarily belong. Since I have spent the last twenty years involved in curriculum development in these fields, it was familiar territory for me, exciting and challenging to draw these concerns together again for a new audience and new times. I was also struck by how yesterday's good practice becomes today's recent history and thus needs constantly to be reforged.

The wide-ranging work carried out in the 1980s by initiatives such as the World Studies 8-13 Project (Hicks, 1990) and the Centre for Global Education had a truly national impact. Between them these two operated in about two-thirds of the LEAs (Local Education Authorities) in England and Wales. But the educational trends of the last six years marginalised much of that excellent work. The global imperative stays the same, but we now fight on new ground, to renew (as this book illustrates) our contacts, networks and impetus. Students now training to be teachers need to know about the new educational movements of the 1980s (Lister, 1987) and how they can nourish a renaissance of radical education today. From old roots come new shoots.

When I talk to my students or read their comments about the course, I am always reaffirmed in the appropriateness of such an approach to education. In essence these students are saying, 'Yes, these issues really matter. Why has no one told us about them before? Yes, education has an important role to play in all this. Show us the resources we can use'. I have a strong sense of *deja vu* and recall my first job in Initial Teacher Education at Charlotte Mason College of Education in the mid-70s. That was what students said then and it is what they are saying today. This is one of the things that stays the same.

Looking forwards

This chapter has described only the first module of International Education and Change, all that has been taught so far at the time of writing. A range of further modules, as outlined at the start of this chapter, will also become available. Two which will take further some of the themes in IE101 are Education for Sustainability, and Environmental Issues: Reflection and Action, which will explore initiatives aimed at creating a more ecologically sustainable future.

I see these modules as being firmly rooted within the tradition of world studies/global education. Good global education both transforms those involved with it and self-reflexively transforms its own practice. What makes the 1990s different is firstly a growing interest in the future, fuelled by the approaching millennium, and secondly, an emphasis on sustainability as a crucial key concept (Bowers, 1993). Much of the most innovative practice today takes place under headings such as 'education for the future' and 'education for sustainability'.

As David Orr (1993) argues:

> Students in the next century will need to know how to create a civilisation that runs on sunlight, conserves energy, preserves biodiversity, protects soils and forests, develops sustainable local economies and restores the damage inflicted on the Earth. In order to achieve such ecological education we need to transform our schools and universities.

We cannot change the world without changing ourselves. In changing ourselves and engaging in action with others we can help initiate the wider sociocultural changes needed to bring about a more sustainable future in the twenty-first century.

CHAPTER 13

Partnership in Action: Bringing Central America into the Primary Curriculum

Sheila J. Bennell, Patricia Daniel and Cynrig E. Hughes

Introduction

This chapter describes a joint project undertaken by staff of the Education Department of Coleg Normal, Bangor, the Môn and Arfon Central America Group, the World Education Project, University of Wales Bangor, and two Gwynedd primary schools. Its aims were to introduce student teachers to the principles of development education and to its place in the study of Central America; to allow them to explore different methods of bringing Central America and development education into appropriate areas of the National Curriculum, including themework; to introduce relevant resources to teachers and student teachers; to help pupils develop their understanding of Central America through various kinds of creative work; and to further encourage schools to integrate both an awareness of global

issues in general, and Central American studies in particular, into the curriculum.

The result was a stimulating exchange of ideas and interests culminating in student/ pupil workshops, which provided a rounded experience of global education to all the participants.

The members of the partnership

The teacher educator:
Cynrig Hughes

Coleg Normal is an old-established College of Higher Education which offers BEd courses through the medium of Welsh and English. The third and fourth year students have an opportunity to enrol on optional courses with the aim of deepening their interest and understanding in various areas. The Multicultural course is one of these and it builds upon the awareness element contained in an earlier course 'The School and Society' and on the Welsh National Curriculum's cross-curricular theme 'Community Understanding'. It aims to provide a general background to the multi-ethnic nature of British society and to introduce students to second language learning techniques, development education and curriculum materials.

One of the key elements in the course is the emphasis that is placed upon the consequences of stereotyping. Much of the work involves discussions regarding how teachers can help children to move beyond the prevailing stereotypes that can limit their horizons. Students are encouraged to think of strategies that will enable children to question the stereotypes produced by social groupings. Furthermore, it is important not only to look at cultural diversity in our own country but also to consider the global aspect. The inclusion of Development Education as one of the central themes of the course can help students in this task. There is a definite need for them to work with children in order to tackle the over-simplified generalisations that are commonly made about the developing world.

Staff at the World Education Project in Bangor are ideally placed to help me do this, thanks to their knowledge of the issues, their experience with children and the resources at their disposal. Their involvement in the course gives the students an opportunity to see the different ways in which they can work with children in order to get past the stereotypes of poverty to the real people of developing countries.

The development educators

The World Education Project: *Sheila Bennell*

This Development Education Centre, established in 1983 and funded by Christian Aid and Oxfam, is based within the Welsh National Centre for Religious Education in the University of Wales, Bangor. The Project members work closely with both primary and secondary teachers and pupils (through in-service training and in school-based projects) and with students and staff in Higher Education, to promote the inclusion of a global perspective throughout education. One of the benefits of being situated in the RE Centre is that the Project has been able to accrue a large resources collection, housed within its Library, which is available to teachers for loan. The integral bookshop can order materials and is widely used by teachers throughout Wales. Students of Coleg Normal, situated within a mile of the Centre, therefore have a wide variety of resources available to them.

We find that teachers are often unaware of resources and unsure about how to tackle the study of other countries in a positive way. If we can introduce the BEd students to the variety of resources and to ways of using them at this early stage of their careers, they will begin to reap the rewards as soon as they move out to teach full-time in schools. We have already seen the fruits of this training: former students contact us for information and help and turnover of resources in the lending system is rapidly increasing.

The Môn and Arfon Central America Group: *Patricia Daniel*

Established in 1988 with the aims of promoting issues of peace and social justice in Central America and the Caribbean and of providing a local platform for Central American culture and arts, the group's work with schools has been supported by a grant from Christian Aid. When working with schools our aim is to raise local awareness about Central America among both teachers and pupils, to involve young people in Central America human rights issues and to promote links with young people in Central America. We work with teachers across all age ranges: for example, the workshops with student teachers described below followed a Sixth Form day held in the autumn, which attracted about sixty students from four schools. Our aims are to help the younger generation in North Wales develop a commitment and sense of responsibility towards the Central America region in particular and, more generally, a willingness to look beyond their national borders.

Central America is a useful area to study for several reasons. It is a particularly good example of the influence of economic and political intervention by countries of the North on development, stability and environment of countries of the South. It provides the opportunity to examine the positive aspects of what is usually dismissed as a disaster area, where its peoples have in the past and continue still to come up with creative and courageous solutions to serious social problems. There are also many historical parallels between Central America and Wales, for example, in the exploitation by outsiders of their natural resources and in the fight to preserve their language and culture and to regain autonomy.

The schools and children

The two schools which took part in 1994 provided an interesting range of opportunities and contrasts: one was in a nearby town and the other a small village; one school used Welsh as the main teaching medium and the other mainly English; both schools normally used a thematic approach to curriculum planning; both schools had already worked with the college; the staff of both schools are always open to new ideas and approaches; the head teachers indicated that they needed guidance to extend their thematic work in the field of development education.

Introducing the students to development education

> If we change ourselves we change the world (Confucius).

The Central America workshops took place over a period of four weeks at the end of the multicultural course. For several years the development education portion of the course has been led by members of the the World Education Project. The aim to familiarise students with some of the key issues of development education and associated teaching approaches, techniques and materials. The workshops are organised at two levels: the students' and the children's. The student workshops are designed so that students experience a working situation similar to that of the primary school.

They are expected to evaluate published materials, plan a theme, and produce classroom-based materials appropriate to the children's age and ability. The two preliminary sessions, with students alone, lasted for one and a half hours each and were conducted in both Welsh and English. The final two sessions, which included the primary school pupils, each lasted for three hours.

These joint workshops, when local schools bring children aged 7-11 to the college over a period of two to three weeks, focus on the micro aspects of teaching rather than whole class organisation. Students work in pairs with a group of children to develop an aspect of the current class theme, in a safe and supportive situation, alongside tutors, teachers and fellow students. They are encouraged to experiment with a variety of techniques and strategies; to ensure a sequence of development education activities over a period; to respond to ideas offered by the teachers and children; and to report back to class teachers, tutors and fellow students on work achieved.

Introducing development education and Central America

The first session introduces Development Education; its background, rationale, methodologies and place in the curriculum. We aim to help them understand:

☐ the interdependence of nature, people and nations and the lack of a boundary between local and global;

☐ the value of diversity and different cultures;

☐ the importance of understanding and questioning the role of change;

☐ that children's natural interest is a good starting point.

Using extracts from *The School is Us* (Renton, 1993) students brainstormed what knowledge, attitudes and skills they would like their pupils to possess when they left school. On the practical side, we offered examples of how development education can be brought into the curriculum successfully and of different methods of planning themework, including the Development Compass Rose developed by Birmingham DEC (see Figure 1). Since many of these students will be working in Wales, we introduced them to the Welsh development education group, Cyfanfyd, whose members come from institutions of Higher Education and development NGOs working in close liaison. Cyfanfyd had a display of development education materials in the college library over the period of the workshops.

The topic of Central America was introduced to the students through:

☐ a brainstorm/quiz on the area;

☐ location/mapwork;

☐ videos, slides, poetry and music;

☐ first-hand accounts in children's creative work from Central America (including pictures of war scenes drawn by Salvadorian refugee children in Honduras);

☐ project work from two London schools undertaken with Amnesty International and local church and refugee groups, which had lead to a wide range of classroom work including creating a newsletter and writing to the families of the

Development Compass Rose (see Development Education Centre, 1995)

*N*atural

These are questions about the environment - energy, air, water, soil, living things and their relationships to each other. These questions are about the built as well as the 'natural' environment.

*W*ho decides?

These are questions about power, who makes choices and decides what is to happen; who benefits and loses as a result of these decisions and at what cost.

*E*conomic

These are questions about money, trading, aid, ownership, buying and selling.

*S*ocial

These are questions about people, their relationships, their traditions, culture and the way they live. They include questions about how, for example, gender, race, disability, class and age affect social relationships.

disappeared (Burr, 1992 and Jones, 1993);

☐ discussion about the United Nations Convention on the Rights of the Child and statistics of Human Rights violations in Central America.

The list of the materials used (see Appendix, pp.119-120) is a comprehensive summary of resources for teaching about Central America. (See also Daniel and Bennell (1995) for a fuller account of these workshops.)

Incorporating Development Education and Central America into class themes

Students spent the second session planning for work with the primary school pupils. They were given a theme web with suggestions of topics which could incorporate studies of Central American life and culture and a guide to how subject areas of the National Curriculum could be covered. (See Bennell and Daniel, op. cit.). Topics were chosen to fit in with the schools' current themework titles: *Important Days, Flight, Trees* and *The Weather*. Issues tackled ranged from the effect on pre-Columbian civilisations of the Spanish Conquest to the present situation of refugees and the disappeared. Some students focused on aspects of everyday life and work, arts and crafts.

A wide variety of resources was available, including a collection of artefacts from Mexicolore, which provided the opportunity for using authentic clothes and toys for drama work, demonstrating traditional cooking methods with kitchen equipment and illustrating the skills and uses of weaving. One group was able to pilot a new computer software package on the Aztecs (Sherston Software, 1993), which involved active work by pupils on the Aztec calendar, Aztec naming systems (dependent on the time a person is born) and Aztec writing.

Working with the children

During the following two weeks the students worked in pairs with small groups of KS2 children who enthusiastically produced a wide range of work which they later displayed in their schools. They made *papier mache* masks and musical instruments which used natural resources, inspired by the Mexican festival, Day of the Dead (topic *Important Days*). They presented a drama simulation of the flight of refugees from their country and their journey to a safe haven (*Flight* and see 'Journeys' in Rutter, 1992), and made a colourful collage map to summarise the information learned in a study of changes in afforestation in the Americas over the last century (*Trees*). One group compared village life in Guatemala with life in a village in North Wales — food, work, play, houses. Another project involved designing and weaving friendship bracelets using traditional weaving boards. Students discussed the effects of natural disasters in the region with children, who then created the front page of a newspaper with headlines, reports and pictures. Yet another group produced posters based on their work on the missing in Guatemala, including poems and pictures.

Their teachers watched the work in progress and expressed interest in hearing about follow-up opportunities, including availability of resources and help in the area.

Evaluation and outcomes

The students

The students' evaluation forms confirmed that they had enjoyed the experience. They felt that they had certainly learned a great deal about Central America, about which many knew little beforehand, and that they were more aware of the issues there and, importantly, of ways to teach about them. As one student said:

> I didn't know much about Central America before the workshops but I was looking forward to them with curiosity and interest. I found them very enjoyable indeed and learned a lot and I am enthusiastic about being involved further in Central American issues.

They felt, however, that they would have been more relaxed if the sessions had been earlier in the year, away from exam pressure.

The development educators

From the point of view of the **World Education Project**, our own practice was enhanced as we deepened our knowledge about Central American issues, making it easier for us to advise on future work relating to this region of the world. Working with students, local schools and the Central America Group gave us an opportunity to experiment with different ways of introducing a 'distant locality'. We hope to receive feedback over the years as we see how subsequent student teachers tackle the classroom challenge of introducing new regions of the world into the curriculum.

Learning about and from Central America was not confined to the students and teachers who took part in these sessions. Much of the work by pupils of Ysgol Deiniolen was lent for display at an all-Wales Development Education Conference and a North Wales Central America Conference. Two Welsh/English publications have made the work accessible throughout Wales (Daniel and Non Parri, 1994; Daniel and Bennell, 1995). These have been welcomed by local teachers, advisers and NGO workers. 'I'd like to emphasise the importance of Welsh medium educational products as these are very limited at the present time, Elenid Jones, Secretary for Education, Cymorth Cristnogol/Christian Aid, Wales.

Following the workshops and a subsequent visit to Nicaragua, the **Môn and Arfon Central America Group** have set up links between schools there and schools in Gwynedd. We have chosen this area (on the Atlantic coast of Nicaragua) because there are several linguistic minority groups and an established bilingual intercultural education programme. Year 5 pupils of one local school have, as part of their themework on communications, started writing letters to their bilingual counterparts in Nicaragua and raising money to help provide basic equipment. As far as the Central America Group is concerned, this project enabled us to make contact with a range of people involved in education in the area and has raised our profile as an educational resource.

The Teacher Educator

For a tutor responsible for the College course, it was encouraging to see the students attempting to put into practice ideas which were discussed during seminar work. Much of the work that takes place on the course is theoretical and it is not always easy for me to follow this up into the classroom. The pupil workshop situation gave me an insight into how my students would respond to ideas and theories in the teaching/learning context. I took particular pleasure in seeing the students using key principles discussed earlier in the term. Published materials were available but these were used carefully and intelligently to fit a purpose identified by the students. I felt that the students made imaginative and original responses to the topics and on the whole succeeded in planning a series of relevant experiences in order to deepen children's understanding. I hope that these students, having had this experience, will have the confidence to plan similar work in the future and will take these ideas with them into their teaching lives.

This multi-agency collaboration showed that it is possible to incorporate Central America and global issues into class themes. It raised awareness at various levels and it confirmed that young children are capable of taking on board complex human rights issues as well as appreciating cultural diversity. It provided an opportunity for experimentation and a means of disseminating practical ideas to schools. But most importantly in the context of the issues raised by this book, it demonstrated the potential for successful partnership in Initial Teacher Education — between Higher Education, teachers, and education workers in NGOs a partnership that enables student teachers to explore the practical possibilities of becoming global teachers.

Appendix

GENERAL INFORMATION

Christian Aid (1986) *In a Strange Land — Exiles and Migrants*, London: Christian Aid.

Jones, M.G., Daniel P. and Loveluck G.D. (1993) *Community Understanding: A Cross Curricular Theme in Initial Teacher Training*, Bangor: Bangor Monographs, School of Education, University of Wales, Bangor.

Oxford Development Education Centre (1986) *Books to Break Barriers: a review guide to multi-cultural fiction*, Oxford.

Rutter, J. (1992) *Refugees: A Resource Book for 8-13 year olds*, London: Refugee Council.

UN Centre for Human Rights/UNICEF (1990) *Convention on the Rights of the Child*, London: UNICEF.

UNICEF-UK (1991) *We are what we eat, but who controls our choice?* London: UNICEF-UK.

CENTRAL AMERICA

Textbooks and packs

Alforja/El Salvador and Guatemala Committees for Human Rights (1985) *The Missing* (tape slide set based on the song Desaparaciones by Ruben Blades), London: Alforja/El Salvador and Guatemala Committees for Human Rights.

Brennan, J. (1988) *Cooperating with Nicaragua: how a Lancashire school traded with a Nicaraguan cooperative*, Preston: Lancashire Development Education Centre.

Burgos-Debray, E. (1984) *I ... Rigoberta Menchu — an Indian woman in Guatemala*, London: Verso.

Burr, M. (1992) *We Have Always Lived Here — The Maya of Guatemala*, London: Central America Human Rights Coordination.

CAHRC (1992) *Five Hundred Years of Resistance: Central America Campaign Pack*, London: Latin America Bureau.

Clarke, M. (1983) *The Oxfam Recipe Book*, Oxford: Education Department, Oxfam.

Daniel P. and Bennell S. (1995) *Dod a Chanolbarth America i mewn i'r Cwricwlwm Cynradd/Bringing Central America into the Primary Curriculum* (teachers' guide), Bangor: Grwp Canolbarth America Mon/Arfon Central America Group.

Edmonds, J. and Cook, R. (1989) *Each One Teach One: Learning about Nicaragua*, Leeds: Leeds Development Education Centre.

Education Project (1992) *I, Rigoberta* (book, slides and teaching pack), London: Central America Human Rights Co-ordination.

El Salvador and Guatemala Committees for Human Rights/War on Want Campaigns Limited (1985) *Out of the Ashes: The lives and hopes of refugees from El Salvador and Guatemala*, London: El Salvador and Guatemala Committees for Human Rights/War on Want Campaigns Ltd.

El Salvador Committee for Human Rights (1988) *Drawn from Life* (postcards from an exhibition of drawings by refugee children from El Salvador), London: El Salvador Committee for Human Rights.

Guyver, R. (1992) *Christopher Columbus* (topic pack), London: Scholastic Publications/Junior Education.

James, I. (1989) *Mexico*, London: Franklin Watts.

Jarvis, J. (1992) *Introduction to Mexico*, London: UNICEF.

Jones, D. (1993) 'Lost but not forgotten', *Education Network Newsletter*, Autumn 1993 p.3.

Lye, K. (1988) *Nicaragua*, London: Franklin Watts.

Lye, K. (1989) *Central America*, London: Franklin Watts.

Museum of Mankind (1993) *The Skeleton at the Feast: The Day of the Dead in Mexico* (teachers pack), London: Museum of Mankind.

New Internationalist (1991) 'Hidden History: Columbus and the colonial legacy', *The New Internationalist* No. 226, pp.18- 19 and 24-25.

Purkis, S. and Collicot, C. (1992) *Ships and Seafarers* (focus pack), Leamington Spa: Scholastic Publications.

Sherston Software (1993) *Aztecs,* Malmesbury: Sherston Software Ltd.

World University Service (1991) *Where there is no school (Support Central American Education)* (information and poster pack), London.

Stories and poems

Daniel P. and Non Parri L. (1994) *Adlais o America Ladin/ Voices from Latin America/ Ecos de America Latina* (trilingual poetry collection for use in schools), Bethesda: Grwp Canolbarth America Mon/Arfon Central America Group.

Kazantzis, J. (1988) *Poem for Guatemala*: Greville Press.

Pollard, M. (1988) *A New Home for Juanita: a story about Bolivia*, Oxford: Education Department, Oxfam.

Save the Children Fund (1981) *Mr Wolf and his Tail, from Mexico* (Round the World Folk Tales), Basingstoke: Macmillan.

Save the Children Fund (1981) *Tiger and Rabbit, from Puerto Rico* (Round the World Folk Tales), Basingstoke: Macmillan.

Videos

BBC Education (1992) *Columbus 1&2/The Spanish Conquest: Explorers and Encounters*, Landmarks Series 4-6, London: BBC.

BBC Education (1992) *Fifteenth Century World/The Aztecs/ Voyages of Exploration: Explorers and Encounters*, Landmarks Series 1-3, Weatherby, W. Yorkshire: BBC.

Channel 4 (1990) 'The Second Revolution' in *Stolen Childhood: The Rights of the Child; 3, Nicaragua*, London: UNICEF.

Neil, G. (1992) *Explorers and Discoverers*, Factfinders/ Landmarks Series, London: BBC.

Arts, Crafts and Music

Child Education (1990) *Masks*, (project file), Basingstoke: Scholastic Productions.

Deshpande, C. (1988) *Scrape, Rattle and Blow (Friends)*, London: A&C Black.

Deshpande, C. (1993) *Celebrations: World Wide Crafts*, London: A&C Black.

Deshpande, C. (1993) *Food: World Wide Crafts*, London: A&C Black.

East, H. (1989) *Singing Sack*, London: A&C Black.

Ethnographic Resources for Art Education, Advisory Service (1992) *Art of Play: traditional playthings from Africa, Asia, America and Europe*, London: Advisory Service CSV.

Sayer, C. (1989) *Masks*: Pictorial Charts.

McLeod-Brudenell, I. (1986) *Masks (Cross Cultural)*, Nottingham: Nottingham Educational.

Oxfam ( ) *Backstrap Weaving (using Third World Art Forms for Creative Activities)*, Oxford.

Wimbledon Committee for Central America (1985) *Tea and Tortillas: a cookery book for Central America*, Wimbledon.

CHAPTER 14

Global Education in Initial Teacher Education: A Case Study from Ireland

Fionnuala Brennan

Background

In 1987 the Development Education Support Centre (DESC) based in Dublin, Ireland proposed designing and implementing workshops or modules on development education for student teachers at a selection of universities and colleges of education. The following case study is an account of how one of these departments of education responded and how the project has developed over the years. The study provides strong evidence that both students and lecturers judge that a global education module is an important component in initial teacher education.

DESC was established in 1986 by the Irish Department of Foreign Affairs and funded from the (ODA) Overseas Development Assistance budget. The aim of the organisation, based in two teacher education colleges in Dublin

and Limerick, is to raise awareness about development issues. The terms of reference for DESC stress the need to institutionalise development education in the formal education system.

A development education curriculum

As I have argued recently (Brennan et al, 1994), although Development Education (DE) cannot have a single explanatory paradigm, because the cultural, geographical and environmental diversity which exists in different parts of the world leads to different explanations and solutions to basic development problems, there is sufficient agreement among practitioners to come to a working understanding of the term. The most commonly quoted definition (in Hicks and Townley, 1982:9) of DE is that put forward by the United Nations in 1975 which stresses the participation of people in, 'issues of human rights..self reliance and social justice in both developed and developing countries,' based on an understanding of those social, economic and political processes which shape their lives. The Irish Advisory Council on Development Education, (1985) building on this definition, sees it as being concerned with:

> the development of a critical awareness of structures and processes of development operating within and between societies, based on an approach in which the person is an active participant, reflecting on the experience gained and culminating in action.

More recently, recognising the central core and changing context of DE, UNICEF (1992) has renamed it 'Education for Development'. It is described as promoting values of global solidarity, peace and environmental awareness, empowering people with the knowledge and skills to promote these values. Education for development is:

> a learning process which proceeds from knowledge to action. It has evolved from being education about developing countries to a broader concept of education for global citizenship.

Audrey Osler (1994) points to the changing context of DE over the past two decades since the UN definition. The central role of women in development is now recognised, as is the need for a closer relationship between environmental and development education. The influence of educationalists from the South such as the Brazilian educational philosopher, Paulo Freire, (1972) is very much evidenced in its methodology.

An appropriate curriculum for DE should involve a holistic and learner-centred process of empowerment, knowledge of the social, political and economic processes which shape the lives of the learners, a critical analysis of these processes, an understanding of the causes of inequality and of interdependence of people and eco-systems and the development of relevant skills and attitudes which promote action for global solidarity and justice.

Setting up the partnership

The education department of St. Patrick's College, Maynooth, a college of the National University of Ireland, was initially interested in the opportunities which the DESC DE module offered to students for experiential learning and small group work. These appeared particularly attractive in 1987 since, in the previous year, the Government had created the possibility for schools to extend the post-primary cycle by an extra year, from five to six years.

This optional extra year was termed the Transition Year Option, (TYO), and was taken up by many schools around the country. An important aspect of TYO is that a substantial percent of the programme has to be non-core curriculum. The three pillars of the TYO programme are: *Personal Development* (involving Civic, Social and Political Education); *Technical and Academic Development* and *The World of Work*. Active learning methods, cross-curricular approaches and project work are emphasised. Significant gaps in the preparation of teachers for its implementation have been highlighted, so Development/Global Education has much to offer teachers, especially young student teachers during their teaching practice.

A funding scheme administered by DESC on behalf of the Department of Foreign Affairs provided money for pre-service and inservice teacher education courses in DE. This chapter describes how St Patrick's became involved, having applied for and received a grant through this scheme.

Annually, approximately one hundred and fifty post-graduate students attend a one-year Higher Diploma in Education course at St. Patrick's College to qualify as post-primary teachers in various subject areas, including science, mathematics, English, languages, music, economics, religious education, geography and history. During negotiations with the staff of the university, DESC emphasised our need for counterpart training, involving the participation of college staff together with DESC education officers in the delivery of the module, in order to ensure the eventual institutionalising of DE in the college and the integration of the module into the core Higher Diploma in Education course.

Course content and process

The content of the workshop focuses on some basic development issues such as definitions/perceptions of development, causes of poverty and underdevelopment and global economic/trading structures. In a one-day workshop it would be impossible to raise more than the basic issues in the planned presentations and exercises; many other issues such as human rights, environmental degradation, sustainability, peace, hunger/food security, health and so on can be dealt with in lesson planning in the afternoon session. The process of the workshops, like all global education work, is participatory (see Appendix I for Workshop Programme).

The programme introduces the theme of development and underdevelopment, through presentations and structured activities in which participants explore their own definitions and perceptions and share these with others. A central thread is to provide opportunities for listening to different perspectives, to develop listening skills and to encourage group work and participation. These objectives underlie the entire workshop.

Another objective for the day is to provide students with a variety of practical methods and exercises which they can use later in their own classrooms. We include the analysis of photo-language, ranking exercises, role-plays and simulation games, all of which raise development issues. The emphasis is on experiential learning skills and group work.

A very important part of the afternoon programme is the class planning session, during which students work together in subject groups to produce class plans that incorporate a global education perspective in their own subject. The plans should follow the syllabus requirements and be for a specified age and ability group. Science students, for example, have produced class plans on the theme of the effects of polluted water in the South; history students have planned lessons on colonialism seen from the perspective of the colonised, teachers of English have devised classes using literature written in English by Southern authors to explore issues such as racism and stereotyping.

Evolution and development of the Global Education course

In the first year of operation, 1987, the students were provided with a short introduction to the concerns of DE and a rationale for its inclusion in the post-primary school curriculum by a DESC member of staff and by one of the education lecturers. Students were then invited to participate in a voluntary weekend workshop starting on a Friday evening, running for three hours and again for the full day on Saturday. There was immediate interest from the majority of the one hundred students; sixty enrolled, requiring us to run two concurrent workshops. In 1988 all one hundred and twenty diploma students participated and three weekend workshops were organised. Student evaluations from the first two years consistently recommended that the course should form part of the core curriculum for all student teachers in the college and that it should be timetabled during term time, preferably early in the year.

In 1989 St. Patrick's decided to make the module a compulsory part of the core curriculum, rather than an elective or voluntary choice, and to timetable it during the term. The duration of the workshop was therefore cut somewhat, with the loss of the hours from the Friday evening session. However, as students were tired on Friday evenings and as they invariably had to leave by four o'clock on Saturday the one day workshop proved just as effective. Development education was thus integrated into the core curriculum of the Higher Diploma in Education. The continuing counterpart training led to a diminishing role for DESC and the increased involvement of college staff.

A new structure was designed to accommodate up to one hundred and eighty students and to broaden the module. The final decision was to free a complete week during which the course could take place; this was scheduled during Easter vacation, when all students except student teachers were on holiday. On days one and two all the students attended a number of preparatory lectures, given by college staff from the anthropology and geography departments. These included a short introduction to development theories and the causes of underdevelopment. On days three, four and five, day-long workshops were organised for groups of thirty students from different tutorial groups and studying a variety of subjects.

There have been several important developments in the planning and implementation of the module which demonstrate that the content and process of DE is central rather than peripheral in the education of future teachers. Each year since 1987 more staff from the education department have become actively involved in both the planning and organisation of the workshop. DESC in the first year devised the programme, provided the resources and conducted the workshops which were attended by university staff members; in the following year two staff members facilitated a number of sessions and each year since then the college staff have taken a more active role. Since 1993 all the staff, including the Professor of Education, have been involved in conducting workshop sessions. While DESC staff are still involved, our role is as co-facilitators. The programme is agreed by all involved and the administration and provision of materials is done by the college.

Interestingly, the workshop programme has not changed much since 1987. Evaluations have indicated a high level of satisfaction with the content and process and therefore it has not been thought necessary to change the format (see Appendix II). Other changes underline the importance St. Patrick's attaches to the programme. In 1994 the timing was altered to allow the course to take place in December, in response to repeated student requests over the years to schedule it earlier in the academic year. They argued that they would benefit more if they were exposed to the methodology and given the chance to plan classes together earlier in their teacher training and also that they enjoyed meeting their fellow students in a small group, which created a more cohesive and beneficial course atmosphere.

Also in 1994, the title was changed from 'Development Education Workshop' to 'Higher Diploma Experiential Learning Week: Theme: Education For Global Development.' Thus the aims of the outside agency, DESC, and of the college, are married in the new title and the content and

process are clearly identified. This is important in that the value of the module is recognised and it has been successfully integrated into the initial teacher education curriculum by the staff and is thus no longer solely an outside intervention.

Curriculum developments and practice in Ireland during these years have increased the attractiveness and usefulness of global education in initial teacher education. A greater number of second level schools (approximately 60% in 1994) have taken the Transition Year Option) and it seems clear that teachers are open to new ideas, modules and materials; the syllabus for a pilot programme in social, civic and political education contains many global education issues and much of the methodology; the Junior Cycle (from 12-15 years) in post-primary schools has been revised and the subject syllabi are now more open to active learning methodologies and to global development issues.

Evaluation

Our procedures for short-term and formative evaluation of the workshop include:

☐ students listing their expectations at the start. These are revisited over the day and adjustments made if necessary. This models our commitment to ongoing consultation about the learning process;

☐ the students answering a written questionnaire at the end;

☐ the facilitators telling the students whether they feel they've achieved their own objectives. They also hold a further evaluation meeting immediately after the workshop.

The student questionnaire as well as discussions between DESC and the college staff can lead to revisions to the programme.

The chief points of their evaluations show that students:

☐ respond positively to the teaching approach and format of the workshops;

☐ appreciate the non-lecture format, during which they participate in a 'hands-on' process, learning about methods which they feel translate easily into classroom practice;

☐ value the opportunity to co-operative lesson planning in subject areas with fellow students.

☐ Finally and equally important, they generally comment on how much they enjoyed the day, and how much fun they had in the learning!

In 1992 students were surveyed before participating in the workshop to identify their existing knowledge or awareness of development issues. However, this was a time-consuming process: the questionnaire was lengthy, as there were over a hundred replies to analyse. Given the brevity of a one-day workshop which concentrated largely on process, it would be unreasonable to expect any significant increase in knowledge about development issues so it was decided that a survey was not very valid as an indicator of changing opinions and values. A more useful pro-course investigation and one which could be directly linked to their experience during the Higher Diploma Experiential Learning Week, would

focus on their attitudes about the inclusion of such issues in various subject areas and/or prior awareness of experiential teaching/learning strategies.

It has not been possible to engage in any longer-term follow-up to discover whether the DE input has had any impact on the students' later practice as teachers because it is difficult to keep track of them. Resource packs and catalogues of classroom materials are provided at St. Patrick's for all the students and subsequent requests for resources have been received by DESC from former participants, which suggests that they are doing some global education in the classroom.

Conclusion

The above case study indicates that there are several prerequisites to ensure the success of and to sustain a module on global education in an initial teaching education curriculum. These are:

☐ the course or module should be seen as enriching the students' teaching skills;

☐ it should respond to curriculum changes;

☐ it should be clearly linked with subject syllabi;

☐ qualified staff from a DE centre or NGO should have a good knowledge of both the curriculum and teaching practice, and preferably have classroom experience themselves;

☐ joint planning and responsibility for the programme should be shared by the outside agency and the college staff members;

- ☐ the module should be an essential part of the core curriculum in which all students participate;

- ☐ it should ideally be timed to take place early enough in the academic year to benefit the students' teaching practice;

- ☐ it should be conducted in workshop sessions of no more than thirty participants, to allow for maximum participation, group work practice and time for feedback;

- ☐ the staff of the outside agency should work with the college staff as counterparts until the college becomes self-sufficient;

- ☐ some seed funding, provided by either the development agency or a government department, assists the implementation of the module by offsetting some of the extra costs, such as the purchase of resource materials;

- ☐ the sustained interest and co-operation of the college staff is essential to the continuation of a module on global education in teacher education courses and its integration into the core curriculum of such courses.

Our case study experience proves that not only is it possible to integrate DE into the curriculum but that it is a valued and indeed necessary component in initial teacher education.

Books recommended to students

Hammond, J. (1991) *A Global Curriculum?: Development Education and the Junior Certificate*, Dublin: Curriculum Development Unit/Trocaire.

Greig, S., Pike, G. and Selby, D. (1987) *Earthrights: Education as if the Planet Really Mattered*, London: WWF/Kogan Page.

Pike, G. and Selby, D. (1989) *Global Teacher, Global Learner*, Sevenoaks: Hodder and Stoughton.

Steiner, M. (1993) *Learning from Experience: Co-operative Learning and Global Education*, Stoke on Trent: Trentham Books.

Appendix I

Programme for Higher Diploma in Education Experiential Learning Week 13-15 December 1994

Theme: Education for Global Development

Each year, as part of the Higher Diploma in Education, the Department devotes a week exclusively to the development of experiential/active learning skills. This is a most important element of the course. Just as important as the skills/ methodologies is the theme used to develop them: Education for Global Development. Our world is characterised by the increasing interdependence and interconnectedness of people, subjects and places. This interconnectedness is explored in Education for Global Development through the medium of experiential learning for student teachers in all subject areas. The programme also focuses closely on the classroom applications of Education for Global Development in all subject areas. The programme will be facilitated by Department staff in collaboration with staff from DESC.

PROGRAMME

09.00
What is Development/Global Education?
lecture

09.30
Introductions

09.45
Group expectations/concerns about the workshop
discussion

10.15
Images of development
photo-language

10.45
Causes of poverty
ranking exercise

11.15
Coffee

11.30
The Trading Game
simulation game

12.30
Feedback
discussion

13.00
LUNCH

14.00
Icebreaker
game

14.15
Review of strategies
discussion

14.30
Class planning in subject groups
groupwork

16.00
Presentations

16.15
Evaluation

16.30
Close of programme

Appendix II

Evaluation of Higher Diploma in Education Workshop on Development Education, 1993

The evaluation was collated from 160 forms returned by participating students at the end of the workshops. Six one-day sessions were organised for the entire group of 180 students from all subject areas, with approximately 30 students attending each workshop. Students were given forms asking them to state their main points of criticism/praise of the workshop and their recommendations to improve future ones. They were also asked to rate the workshop from 1 (unsatisfactory) to 5 (excellent).

All comments are noted in this synopsis; however, repititions are only given once. A better representation of the total response would be provided by noting how often certain points were made. In this sense the evaluation is not balanced and future synopses will reflect the total response.

Average rating: 4 out of 5

Positive comments: very useful, well presented, varied, creative approach, practical active learning, enjoyable, good cross- curricular teaching ideas, global aspect good methodology, lesson planning very useful, experiential learning for teacher and students alike, fun while learning, games, sharing ideas, participants' feedback encouraged, a different approach to teaching.

Negative comments: confusion at outset re relevance to my subject, long, demanding day, too much packed in, did not know what to expect, over-evaluation of game, not enough time for some topics, too linked to geography.

Recommendations: more games, more time, fewer lesson plans, provide sample lesson plan applying development education perspective in language class, more role play, provide list of classroom resources.

CHAPTER 15

'The Children Were Beginning to Construct a Revised Image of India': Student Teachers Becoming Global Teachers

Julia Tanner

Introduction

This chapter takes the form of a case study; a 'snapshot' of student teachers' learning as they explore and extend primary children's perceptions of distant places and peoples. I hope to show how such work offers opportunities for the students to begin developing some of the knowledge, understandings, skills and attitudes of the 'global teacher' (Pike and Selby, 1988). By this I mean teachers who are willing and able to provide children with educational experiences which will prepare them to be active and responsible citizens of an interdependent and fast changing world.

The chapter is divided into three sections. The first briefly describes the

background and context of the student teachers' work, while the second presents and analyses the case study material, drawing on student project reports, observations, lesson notes and session evaluations. In the final section, I discuss the students' learning in relation to their development as global teachers.

Background and context

The arguments for student teachers in initial training to develop an understanding of the meanings and implications of global education are compelling, both for the future quality of life and possibly the very survival of humankind, which may well depend on today's children and young people acquiring what Hicks and Tawney (1982) have termed 'global literacy' and developing the ability to think, feel and act from a global perspective (Cogan, 1982).

Geography as a subject area offers unique opportunities for both student teachers and young children to develop a global perspective, because it is centrally concerned with the relationship between people and places on local, national and global scales. Indeed, the recent International Charter for Geographical Education (Commission on Geographical Education, IGU, 1992) argues that:

> geographical education is indispensable to the development of responsible and active citizens in the present and future world...(and)... students require increasing international competence in order to ensure effective cooperation on a broad range of economic, political, cultural and environmental issues in a shrinking world (Commission of Geographical Education IGU, 1992 p.3).

This places education for global citizenship at the very heart of geographical work in schools, colleges and universities.

The relationship between the subject area of Geography as a whole and world studies/global education has been widely explored (Hicks, 1979; Huckle, 1983; Fien and Geber, 1988; Serf and Sinclair, 1992; Catling, 1993; Hopkin, 1994). Here I am concerned with the specific opportunities offered by the requirement of the original Statutory Orders (DES 1991) that all children in Key Stage One and Key Stage Two should study places beyond the UK. Before the National Curriculum, few primary children had opportunities to study distant places, since most geographical work, where it was undertaken at all, concentrated solely on the local area. HMI (1989) reported an almost total absence of a national or global dimension in primary geography, though they were able to find isolated examples of good practice. Many primary teachers, especially early years specialists, were skeptical of the value of the study of distant places — regarding it as too removed from children's everyday life and experience. In addition, few suitable resources and little guidance and advice were available. Thus many primary teachers approached the prospect of teaching distant places with little commitment or confidence. The most recent Ofsted survey found this aspect of the geography curriculum still neglected in schools, reporting that in 1992-3, 'too little attention was given to studying places away from the local area' (Ofsted, 1993, p12).

Children's images and perceptions of distant peoples and places provide a valuable starting point for the 'locality' studies required by the National Curriculum. But, as Wiegand's (1993) review of the research evidence shows, the relationship between knowledge and perception of distant places is complex, and attitudes and images may well be formed in advance of children having much actual information.

Goodey's (1973) model of 'the child in information space' provides a very useful guide to considering children's knowledge and understanding of places. It differentiates between those places of which they have direct, first-hand experiences, and those which they know of and about through vicarious, second-hand experience. It shows children located in their own 'personal space', their immediate home environment, from which they make excursions into the wider world when, for example, they attend school, go shopping, visit the park or are taken on holiday. As children grow older, this known, experienced world expands, as does their knowledge of places acquired from secondary sources such as television, books and picture postcards. Thus the model illustrates the process by which each child develops a unique 'personal geography' based on their individual experiences, information received from second-hand sources and their perceptual abilities and inclinations. Children's perceptions of distant places are a significant component of their personal geographies.

The following case study is based on close analysis of eight final year projects written by primary B.Ed. students in the early 1990s. All were white, six were young women in their early twenties and the other two, a man and a woman, a decade older. These students had all taken Geography as a main elective subject, and had been introduced to active experiential approaches to primary geography and the importance of children's personal geographies as a starting point for geographical work. All chose a 'distant place' focus for their final year classroom project, which is an action enquiry designed to enable students to demonstrate their elective subject knowledge and understanding

and their ability to synthesise work undertaken in professional studies and specialist pedagogy courses. Analysis of and reflection on the children's learning and their own professional development are integral components of this project, so the final reports offer considerable insights into students' developing thinking and understanding.

The case study: exploring and extending children's images of distant places and peoples

The students all chose to start their classroom work by exploring an aspect of children's personal geographies — their initial perceptions of the places they had chosen to study. This approach enables teachers to find out what children already 'know' and also provides useful baseline assessment material. Work on perceptions and images is also seen as a crucial aspect of global and development education (eg Hicks and Steiner, 1989; Development Education Centre, 1990) since it can help young people to become more aware of and sensitive to the effects of bias, and to understand how stereotyped images in the media harm all members of the world community (Fountain, 1995).

The students used a wide range of techniques to elicit children's initial perceptions, including brainstorming, discussion, drawing pictures, responding to or sorting photographs and completing checklists or other predetermined response sheets. Most students used two or three different approaches, recognising that this would give a fuller picture of the children's initial views. They presented comprehensive evidence of the children's responses to the tasks through detailed notes of their observations, transcripts of discussions and conversations, and examples of children's work.

Brainstorming with individuals or groups was used in five of the projects. In some cases the student acted as scribe, or supported the process by asking questions. Lucy reports that even though she was anticipating stereotyped or negative views, she was 'surprised by the extent of the bias exposed in their language'. The transcript of the discussion which took place reveals not only the children's perceptions of India, but also Lucy's skill in eliciting the children's views and encouraging them to develop and expand their answers.

Teacher: I'm going to write down on this piece of paper all the things we can think about. What was your first thought, Emily?

Emily: Well, I think they're poor because they don't have a lot of food. (Teacher writes).

Teacher: Anything else ... (pause). What makes you say that they are poor ... how do you know?

Emily: If you watch the news a lot ... it's on the news if there's a country... they sometimes show you countries far away ... if they're having wars.

Teacher: Do you think that India has wars?

Sarah: A bit ... sometimes.

Carol: They're too poor to buy guns ... if they don't have enough money to buy food. Then if they did get money they wouldn't want to spend it on guns.

Teacher: OK ... What do you think the weather is like in India?

Emily: I think it might be hot ... yeah, dead sunny.

Teacher: How do you think people travel around the country of India?

Susan: They travel around on foot.

Teacher: Do you think all the people travel on foot?

Susan: No ... no some people go in cars.

Angela: They can't travel in taxis, they haven't got enough money to hire taxis.

Susan: The richest ones there, which isn't very rich really, well, they have enough to spare so they cart food around in carts to sell to people.

Simon: Yeah, like lemons and that.

Teacher: OK. What sort of jobs do you think people have? You mentioned people selling food, what do other people do, do you think?

Simon: They don't have jobs.

Emily: They might make food, though.

Susan: How can they make food if they haven't got any money to buy the ingredients?

Emily: Well, I mean corn in the fields and that.

These same inaccurate and negative perceptions were also found in children's drawings of India. Tina, working with a Y2 group, transported them to India on a 'magic carpet'. The children responded well to this role-play:

> pointing out to each other features that they imagined they could see, such as towns, oceans and deserts; and two even reported they could feel the wind blowing the carpet around!

Once safely landed, the children were asked to draw the place in which they had arrived. Their resultant pictures and discussion showed that:

> most of the children thought that Indian people lived in huts or tents ... A hot sun figured in several of the pictures ... All the children thought India was very hot and dry, and that there was a permanent drought and food shortage.

The students who used photograph activities found that this approach offered considerable insight into children's knowledge and perceptions (see Appendix I). Janice, working with another group of Y4 children, gave them 32 photographs to sort into 'India/not India' groups. Of the 16 Indian photographs, depicting a variety of places and situations, only those of the Taj Mahal, an elephant giving rides, and a rural scene were correctly identified. The student was most surprised by the children's dismissive response to urban street scenes:

> That's not India, it's too rich ... Yeah, look at that building (Pointing to a skyscraper in the background) ... And there's cars and stuff ... They use elephants instead of cars, don't they.

This same group dismissed an Indian beach resort scene as 'the Caribbean'. Janice suggested that despite having seen in the atlas and on the globe that India is largely surrounded by sea, 'they did not associate the picturesque coastal scenes with what they imagined to be an entirely dirty and poor country.'

A second student found that a variation of 'Kim's Game', where two children had to remember and describe a photograph to other children who had not seen it, provided useful information about both what the describers 'saw' and what the listeners imagined from the description they heard. These two children, describing a photograph of an Indian farmer with bullocks, told their partners:

> There's a man in the picture and he's brown, there's some animals and it's sunny... The man's happy... There's some trees and a milk churn next to the man and a drink in case he gets hot... And he's got a turban on.

When shown the picture, one child responded:

> It's not what I thought it would look like ... I didn't know that man was going to be African.

Another way of using photographs is to pose direct questions. Simon used this approach with some photographs of Kirua in Tanzania, asking eg. 'Where do you think these children live?' and 'What is it like there?' He found that in some cases children's preconceptions seemed to prevent them from really seeing the photograph — as in this conversation stimulated by one of the photographs:

Colin: The children in this picture are poor.

Teacher: How can you tell?

Colin: Because they're not wearing shoes.

(Children in photo were playing a game and had removed their shoes which were on the ground near them.)

Teacher: Do you think they have enough to eat?

Colin: No, I think they are hungry.

(Some of the children in the picture were eating.)

The students' accounts and analyses of these initial activities show that they were able to experiment with an imaginative range of techniques to elicit children's initial perceptions. In the teaching that followed, most developed the work by using one of the published 'locality' packs as the core resource for their project. While they used some of the activities suggested in the packs, eg caption matching, they also developed their own ideas, used atlases and globes to locate the places studied, and a range of picture, story and information books to help the children place the locality in its regional and national context. Some groups were also able to handle and work with artefacts, listen to appropriate music, cook and eat relevant food, or meet with someone with personal first-hand knowledge of the place. The projects provided ample evidence that these first-hand experiences motivated the children and helped them to develop a richer understanding of the lives of the people in the locality they were studying.

Student teachers learning to become global teachers

Here, however, I am concerned not with the children's learning but with that of the student teachers. I have suggested that the experience of exploring children's perceptions of distant places offered them opportunities to develop some of the knowledge, understandings, skills and attitudes of global teachers, and now return to this proposition. I believe that the major significance of this work lies in the student teacher's engagement with the children's perceptual worlds — 'the world as they perceive it to be and the images they hold of it' (Catling, 1993, p 344). Exploring children's personal geographies proved to be a powerful learning experience for the student teachers, forcing them to acknowledge the implications for their teaching.

In terms of knowledge and understandings, these students learnt a great deal about children's perceptions of African and Asian countries. They found that children do have some knowledge, but that this tends to be partial, inaccurate and often stereotyped. Although their reading (of eg Bale, 1987; Wiegand, 1992) had led them to expect this, many were nonetheless surprised and shocked by the nature and consistency of the children's perceptions:

> The children had very stereotyped images of Indian people and India as a whole. They thought that the country was hot and dry. In fact their image of India fitted perfectly into what Wiegand (1992) found, that for those children who had not travelled to India it was a place that was hot and dry, where people ate rice and curry and lived in 'huts' amongst herds of elephants.

Another benefit of such work is that it places student teachers in direct contact with children's attitudes, providing opportunities for them to reflect on the significance of the affective domain in geographical work. Through careful observation and analysis of the children's responses to the initial tasks, they detected some stereotypical images and misconceptions, and recognised that these revealed underlying attitudes and values. Most of the students recognised from the outset the need to engage with the affective domain and to challenge or extend children's images where these were negative or partial. Some display considerable understanding of the need to deal sensitively and constructively with children's existing views, using them as a starting point. A good example is found in Penny's work. She chose to focus on the issue of hunger and anticipated correctly that the children would feel great sympathy and concern for individuals affected by famine but would nonetheless see them as hapless and helpless victims of a natural

disaster. Thus she recorded that subsequent work would have simultaneously 'to build on positive aspects of the children's perceptions' while also 'challenging their values and attitudes'.

The students expressed concern at the children's negative perceptions and wondered at the outset how much they would be able to encourage the children to modify their views and opinions. Simon, writing after completing the initial activities, reflected that:

> There was evidence in the things children said that the images they see on television are very strong, and remain with them even in spite of contrary evidence ... It was obvious that the overwhelming impression ... was that African people are all poor and a lot of them are starving. This impression stayed with them even when they were shown pictures of apparently healthy, happy and well-fed children... all of the children commented that the children were hungry, even though they looked well fed, indeed one of them in the photograph was shown eating ...it demonstrates, I think, that children need a lot of evidence presented to them if they are to overcome their preconceptions.

One very positive aspect of this work, however, is that on the whole student teachers learnt that the children were very interested in the work and open to new ideas. Ruth reports of the Y3 children with whom she worked:

> The group clearly proved to me that they were capable and ready to understand and absorb a different

culture. They learned freely without prejudice. It was refreshing to see these children sincerely interested in the lifestyle and the people we studied, unlike so many people within our society today.

Another student teacher overheard the following exchange half-way through the first session when the children were looking at a picture of an Indian woman in an atlas. She recognised it as a significant moment when they engaged with new information and shifted their view:

> — You know we said that people from India were poor — well, this woman doesn't look poor and she's from India.

> — Oh um, she looks rich ...

As she later recorded, it was already evident after only 30 minutes that '*the children were beginning to construct a revised image of India*'.

While some of the student teachers did find initial resistance to information which challenged their preconceptions, most report that by the end of the teaching project the children had substantially increased their knowledge of the places studied, and, in some cases at least, had also developed more positive attitudes. Many asked the children to repeat the initial activities, and they report very interesting results. Janice, for example, repeated the photograph sorting activity and found that the children now immediately recognised the urban street scenes as India.

Lucy:	I didn't think this was India before, but it is.

When I prompted the children to expand on this, I was bombarded with answers:

Lucy:	The animals like we've seen on the video with those funny humps (street cows).
Gavin:	Their clothes are Indian.
Michael:	They have really old-fashioned cars, too, like those.
Lucy:	They still have nice buildings in big cities.

Janice concludes that even over the one week in which she had worked with them, 'the children's knowledge and therefore perceptions of India had changed dramatically'.

There is ample evidence in the reports that the student teachers were developing their teaching skills through experimenting with the active learning techniques associated with global education approaches. They recognised the need to present new and more accurate information, and to give children opportunities to develop empathic understanding of others' lifestyles, cultures and perspectives. There are many glimpses in the project reports of students' emerging understanding of the importance of the 'key ingredients' of the world studies classroom (Steiner, 1993) as they seek to devise learning activities which will help children gain more balanced knowledge and understanding of the localities studied. As the project bibliographies show, many of the tasks were developed or adopted from 'standard' world studies and development education texts (eg Hicks and Fisher, 1985; McFarlane, 1986; Hicks and Steiner, 1989; Development Education Centre, 1990; Fountain, 1990).

In particular, the student teachers show considerable skill in presenting new and more positive images, and in sensitively challenging children's inaccurate perceptions. Rachel's account of introducing some photographs from ActionAid's *Chembakolli* pack describes:

> Before I actually showed the children the pictures, I stressed that they were all of the same village in India. As I suspected, when I actually showed the photographs to the children, Nick said that it was not India, and the other children agreed with him. The reason for this was because the first picture I showed was of the fields and hills around the village. The children did not think that these were India because it was so green … As we went through the photographs, the children picked off familiar features which helped prove to them that the pictures were actually of India. These features include the people and their clothing as well as the buildings.

Two of the students using the *Chembakolli* pack supplemented it with a TV programme *Family and Friends in Delhi* to provide an urban contrast. They found that it had considerable impact. One wrote:

> During the viewing the whole group appeared utterly absorbed by the video and as a consequence responded enthusiastically to the discussion which followed. Many

aspects of the presentation provoked surprise. Comments such as 'they could talk English' and 'they had ice creams' obviously reveal previous misconceptions …

Another, who used a video from the same series which focused on contrasting transport in Britain and in urban and rural India, reported that:

> This audio-visual material was the most effective in changing the children's perceptions of India. It exposes the children to real-life moving images.

The student teachers also show considerable understanding of the importance of helping children develop critical skills in using and interpreting secondary sources. There is evidence in the project reports that the students' own awareness of images of 'economically developing countries' was sharpened by this work, and also that they considered carefully their impact on the children with whom they worked. Exploring the children's original preconceptions was certainly a significant spur. Here is Lucy reflecting on the initial activities:

> The extent to which stereotyping does permeate through the media and resources did surprise me.

Most of the children were offered plenty of activities to help them develop skills in analysing and 'unpacking' images, and in the development of logical thinking and careful use of evidence. The student teachers learnt that children can develop quite sophisticated understanding. Tina reported that one girl, after viewing a television programme which provided contrasting images of India, commented that in future she would consider individual sources of information as 'simply one view'.

The project reports also suggest that the student teachers were beginning to develop some of the core values and attitudes of global teachers. This can be seen in the teaching and learning strategies they choose and also in their belief that primary children's study of distant places can make a contribution to the creation of a better world. In taking the children's initial perceptions as a starting point, they acknowledged the personal nature of children's geographical knowledge and understanding, and demonstrated to the children a respect for their individual opinions and contributions. Subsequent activities were designed to encourage skills in co-operation, critical thinking and reflection and to foster attitudes of open-mindedness, respect for evidence and empathy for people living in distant places. Their evaluations of these activities certainly support Steiner's (1993) finding that teachers feel such approaches can lead to significant learning and attitudinal change.

One of the most striking features of the reports is the student teachers' overwhelming commitment to the view that teaching about distant places can foster respect and tolerance for other people and make a significant contribution to education for international understanding. Many conclude their reports by asserting the value of the study of localities in 'economically developing countries' with primary aged children. Janice speaks for them all when she writes:

I think this investigation was useful and interesting for both the children and myself. The study of distant places is fundamental in exposing children to other cultures and therefore eliminating prejudice resulting from ignorance.

Conclusion

I suggest that this approach to the distant locality studies required by the Key Stage Two National Curriculum for Geography offers considerable potential for fostering student teachers' professional development and understanding. It provides opportunities for them to engage with and reflect on both the person-centred and reconstructionist traditions which underpin global education (Hicks 1994) and to explore their professional response to the challenges of making such work meaningful and relevant to primary aged children. Above all, it seems to strengthen their commitment to education for a better world and to provide them with confidence in their own ability to make a contribution to this work.

Appendix

Selected Visual Resources for Locality Studies

ActionAid (1991) *Chembakolli, A Village in India,* London: ActionAid.

ActionAid (1992) *Pampagrande, A Peruvian Village,* London: ActionAid.

ActionAid (1993) *Nairobi, Kenyan City Lake,* London: ActionAid.

ActionAid (1993) *Pakistan, Change in the Swat Valley,* London: ActionAid.

BBC (1991) Landmarks: Pakistan, London: BBC.

Central Television (1990), *Going Places: Family and Friends in Delhi,* Birmingham: Central Television .

Geographical Association and WorldAware (1992) *Focus on Castries St. Lucia,*Sheffield: Geographical Association and WorldAware.

Geographical Association (1992) *Ladakh: The Tibetan children's village of Choglamsar,* Sheffield: Geographical Association.

Jarvis, H. (1993) *Palm Grove: A study of a locality at Victoria Falls,* Zambia, London: UNICEF.

McFarlane, C. et al (1992) *Where Camels are Better than Cars: a locality study in Mali,* Birmingham: Development Education Centre and London: Save the Children.

Midwinter, C. et al (1992) *Living and Learning in a Tanzanian Village,* Manchester: Manchester Development Education Project.

Oxfam Education (1991) *Gariyahn Transport in Pakistan,* Oxford: Oxfam Education.

CHAPTER 16

Environmental Education for Sustainable Futures: Developing an Action-research Model for Primary Initial Teacher Education

Sue Lyle

Setting the scene

Recent and planned changes to initial teacher education in England and Wales mean that the possibilities of developing critical approaches to the practice of education are becoming restricted. Less time is available for students to engage in reflection and debate about important educational issues as they become more concerned with 'what we do' rather than 'why we do it'. In addition the success or failure of student teachers is determined through assessment of their practice against a detailed list of competences, which also emphasises the 'doing' rather than the 'thinking'. This is a loss to the craft of teaching and also has particular relevance to the field of global education.

This chapter describes recent initiatives in environmental education for sustainable futures in a four year BA (Primary Education) degree. This work developed a model for understanding and planning interdisciplinary environmental education which gave both tutors and students an opportunity to engage with the meanings and methodologies of environmental education (EE) through collaborative working and critical reflection.

Environmental education for sustainable futures:
A political perspective

There has been an increasing international acceptance of the importance of global education, and in particular the part of it described as 'environmental education for sustainable futures' (EESF). Governments and international organisations clearly recognise the seriousness of the global environmental crisis. Preparing 'environmentally educated' teachers who are capable of providing high quality environmental education has been identified as a priority (Unesco-UNEP, 1990). The European Council of Ministers issued a joint statement that environmental education should form part of the education of persons at all levels in education (CoE, 1988). In Britain the Department of the Environment's paper, *Environmental Responsibility: An agenda for further and higher education* (DoE, 1994) locates itself firmly in the context of the environmental crisis facing the planet:

> Every Further and Higher Education institution should adopt and implement an appropriately timetabled and prioritised strategy for the development of environmental education (DoE, 1994).

The task of defining and addressing the critical goals of environmental education has undergone continuous change and development since the Belgrade Charter (UNESCO, 1977), both influencing and being influenced by the growth of public concern about the environment. The term 'sustainability', now widely used by politicians and environmentalists, first emerged in the public arena with the publication of the World Conservation Strategy (IUCN UNEP WWF, 1980) and was later reinforced by the Brundtland Report (WCED, 1987) where it was defined as

development 'which meets the goals of the present without compromising the ability of future generations to meet their own needs'. The 1992 Rio Summit reinforced all this. By drawing our attention to the difficulties facing rural people in the South whose survival options appear to force them to destroy natural resources, these reports showed the links between economic growth, poverty, development and environmental preservation. Thus education for sustainability has become the central goal of environmental education during the 1990s.

> Sustainable living must be the new pattern for all levels: individuals, communities, nations and the world. To adopt the new pattern will require significant change in attitudes and practices of many people. We will need to ensure that education programmes reflect the importance of an ethic for living sustainably (IUCN/UNEP/WWF, 1991).

An educational perspective

Alongside these reports and initiatives has been the work of the critical educators who have developed the rationales and strategies for its practice. Three approaches to Environmental Education have gained currency since the late 1970s: education *about, in* and *for* the environment. Fien (1993) observes that education *about* the environment, which focuses on children's knowledge of the environment and is commonly found in geography and science lessons, is the most prevalent in schools. Education *in* the environment concentrates on the affective domain and takes place outside the classroom, since contact with nature is thought to encourage personal growth and thus develop environmental awareness and concern. Education *for* the environment aims for learners to develop a sense of responsibility towards the environment, and actively to become part of the solution to environmental problems. It therefore includes the development of children's political understanding. Sterling (1990) points to 'holism' as the guiding principle. This combines social responsibility and concern for others with a desire to live in harmony with nature, and emphasises the ecological basis for valuing the interrelatedness of all life forms on the planet. It also promotes values such as sustainability and equality.

This holistic approach has evolved as a result of the integration of environmental education and development education. Often referred to as Environmental Education for Sustainability, it includes all three approaches to EE by incorporating a concern for immediate environmental issues and improvements, and education for sustainability in the long term — a futures perspective.

The Curriculum Council for Wales

The wider political and educational background which informed the Curriculum Council for Wales' (CCW, 1992) advisory paper on environmental education clearly draws on the major international reports and views of critical educators. It defines *environment* as the interaction between our physical surroundings and the social, political and economic forces that we create to organise our lives. This definition unquestionably implies that all human beings are party to environmental problems and may play an active role in solving them. The document's analysis of environmental education puts these perspectives at the heart of the learning process. It is also particularly concerned with the relationships people in different parts of the globe have with the natural world. Thus a legitimate basis for inquiry in environmental education might consider: *how* resources are obtained and used; *who* has access and makes decisions; and the role of *power*, past and present, in those relationships.

Since questions of this nature, which are invariably controversial and emotionally charged, have implications for the kind of teaching which takes place, CCW has identified the teaching processes required for environmental learning under three headings: enquiry and critical reflection; communication; participation and action. The CCW framework provides a firm rationale for classroom investigations into environmental problems in the context of human interaction with the natural world and the way social systems are organised, e.g. pollution, degradation of soils, destruction of natural habitats. It also points towards the personal qualities and the attitudes and values implicit in education for the environment:

☐ a sense of personal responsibility for the environment, locally and globally;

☐ a commitment to action for just and sustainable development for all;

☐ a readiness to evaluate and, possibly, modify one's own lifestyle

☐ and perspectives on environmental issues (CCW, 1992).

Environmental education and Initial Teacher Education: The CCW model

This section describes two initiatives in the Initial Teacher Education programme at Swansea Institute of Higher Education (SIHE), both of which were influenced by the political and educational contexts described above. The first took place in 1992-3 and was supported by the *Thinking Futures* project initiated by the World Wide Fund for Nature (WWF). This was a pilot project with students in their final year of teacher education. The second, in 1993-4, built on this experience and was additionally influenced by the competence-based requirements issued by the Department for Education (DfE 14/93)

1. The Thinking Futures Project 1992-1993

A team of tutors worked together to develop EE in the four year BA (Primary Education) degree, using the perspectives of the CCW Advisory Paper as both rationale and reference point.

The project began by conducting a curriculum audit to assess how far EE was already part of the BA. As a result, a topic about a local issue (*Water in the Swansea Valley*) was planned. This reflected existing course content taught in three separate subject areas, Geography, History, and Science,

bringing them together in an interdisciplinary inquiry and research into three themes. Each of the disciplines was already teaching aspects of the themes separately. These were: the rise and fall of Swansea as a world metal smelting centre, the degradation of the environment due to industrial pollution, and the development of the Lower Swansea Valley Project to make good the damage of the industrial past.

The focus on concrete environmental issues relevant to Swansea therefore gave students the chance to develop their understanding of the concepts and to practise the skills associated with EESF in an experiential way and gain the understanding they needed to form their own judgements about future environmental decision making, and to consider what their own role might be, both personally and in their future careers as teachers. Students were also able to situate the perspectives of EEFS within the context of disciplines such as History, Geography and Science.

Students worked in cross-subject groups to develop classroom materials and were encouraged to consider the pedagogical implications during workshops focusing on curriculum planning. They used a 'Six Stage Planning Framework' which offers a clear progression in the development of both factual and conceptual understanding of all aspects of environmental understanding. This framework incorporates key features of education *in, through,* and *for* the environment.

STAGE 1 Ecological understanding
— how the life-support systems of
the planet work — people as *part* of
the planet, not *apart* from it.

STAGE 2 Aesthetic appreciation —
the beauty of the natural world —
children need to *feel* part of, not
apart from the planet, and not just
understand this intellectually.

STAGE 3 What is happening to the
natural systems of the planet — past
and present, and the people who
depend on them.

**STAGE 4 What are the
consequences?** — now, and in the
future.

STAGE 5 Why is it happening? —
What current beliefs, policies and
practices are either contributing to
the destruction or alleviating it.

STAGE 6 What can we do about it?
— ourselves, locally, in conjunction
with others, or nationally through
the democratic process. What sort
of futures do we want?

Each group was required to produce at
least one activity for each stage. (A
fuller account of this work is found in
Inman, 1995.)

The practical model underpinning
the project can be summarised as
follows:

☐ starts from interdisciplinary/cross
subject tutor and student teams;

☐ enables students to work
collaboratively;

☐ enables students themselves to
learn in an experiential manner and
also to learn how to use experiential
techniques;

☐ introduces the Six Stages of
Environmental Knowledge and
Awareness (above) as the baseline
for planning the content of EE work.

2. Ocean Environments 1993-1994

The new requirements for a
competence-based model (DfE 14/93) of
teacher education and its impact on
course delivery meant that the project
could not run in the same way in
1993/4. Instead a voluntary project was
introduced and final year students were
invited to participate. They were to
work together on a teaching pack on the
theme of *Ocean Environments,* to be
jointly published by SIHE and the Royal
Society for the Protection of Birds
(RSPB). Students were expected to
come to meetings and workshop
sessions in their own time, to plan the
teaching pack and to be jointly involved
in writing the materials. In the event,
twenty four out of a possible forty eight
students specialising in the junior age
range (age 7-11) came forward. Some of
these students were able to pilot the
materials on their final teaching
practice and the results were published
in 1995. Workshops were facilitated by
the author, working voluntarily on top
of a full timetable, and the education
officer of the RSPB.

A Process-based approach

The processes of planning the 'Oceans'
work took into account learning from
the *Thinking Futures* project. That
project had high status because it had
been jointly planned by staff from
different discipline areas as a
compulsory part of the students'
professional training. The style of
educational practice promoted, and the

definitions and meanings ascribed to EESF, had been firmly in the hands of staff. The outcome had included some quality classroom materials, but students had had limited opportunity to explore the theoretical perspectives of environmental education or to reflect on their personal position vis-a-vis these perspectives.

In the more informal setting of a voluntary group, the students could be involved in identifying environmental issues and interrogating the rhetoric of EEFS in order to negotiate agreed meanings for the terminology. During the first two weeks of the project the students were asked to explore what the 'environment' meant to them. Predictably, they identified many of the environmental issues which receive media attention — acid rain, the ozone layer, global warming, rainforest destruction and so on. A programme from the CAFOD series on environmental and development issues (*Greening the Earth* [CAFOD, 1989]) clarified the concepts associated with sustainable development. Subsequent input focused on the more specific topic of oceans and the concerns of the RSPB, as reflected in their *Marine Environment* campaign. Having set the project in a real world context, students were introduced to the EE planning framework and extracts from the CCW Advisory Paper.

These two documents provided the environmental education discourse around which the curriculum development work would take place. Students worked in small groups to explore the documents and, over several weeks, negotiated an agreed interpretation. In the process, they began to develop a principled and critical understanding of the discourse of EESF in the context of planning classroom activities. This exercise in ascribing meaning to terminology was undertaken for the practical purpose of planning and writing classroom materials.

Still using the planning framework, and with reference to the CCW document, the students applied their understanding of EESF to the writing task. The materials they produced were intended for use on their final teaching practice. This meant considering how a critical, process-based approach to teaching could be used, that would meet the requirements of the National Curriculum and the expectations of the teachers with whom they would be working. Discussions often focused on the difficulties of implementing a cross-curricular theme in the context of a curriculum which is becoming increasingly dominated by subject considerations in both planning and implementation.

This perceived problem was 'solved' by developing a subject-focused approach to the planning, concentrating on Science and Geography attainment targets whilst trying to maintain EESF as an overarching aim. In this way students took account of the reality of the classroom setting in which they would be using their materials and used the National Curriculum-determined goals to develop materials whilst meeting their own EESF aims.

The theoretical perspectives which had underpinned their interpretation of the CCW document and the planning tool became more visible to the students in the process of writing their materials.

The subsequent practice in school made them face the constraints of matching theory to practice. Some of the schools felt that the materials would not fit in with existing curriculum plans, others allowed only some of the materials to be used. Only one school allowed the student to take over the whole curriculum for six weeks to implement the project fully. The students' comments tell the tale:

> ...my teacher doesn't believe in the National Curriculum, she's always worked on themes like this and she loved it.

> ...an in-depth consideration of a topic like this takes time if the children are to produce quality work... my teacher said the demands of the National Curriculum means we have to focus on getting through the statutory requirements.

Reviewing and appraising

After teaching practice the students met again to make a critical appraisal of their classroom situations and the use of the materials in the classroom. This process made classroom practice more intelligible in a number of different ways. Their understanding of curriculum planning and constraints on classroom practice had increased as they tried to negotiate classroom time to test out their ideas. They had become more aware of the sets of beliefs and assumptions, they, and the classroom teachers with whom they had worked, held. Their experience of trying to negotiate space for EESF in the curriculum highlighted the gap between what they wanted to do and the reality of classroom contexts:

> ...the problem is, my teacher doesn't like group work... she says it doesn't work with her children...

The joint evaluation of the materials after the classroom practice enabled the students to revisit the theory in light of the practical experience and to clarify their understanding of the theory of EESF and the reality of classroom practice. The practical task of appraising materials in terms of their suitability for the classroom and the age or level of the children focused discussion on an active learning approach to classroom organisation and management

> ...the children really enjoyed the work, they actively tried to make meaning out of the activities... they loved all the new words they learnt.

> ...mine just loved the role-play — it was incredible how sophisticated they were in explaining the range of views people might have on environmental issues.

> ...what doing this has shown me is how important it is to give children the chance to talk about the issues themselves...by talking they develop their understanding.

> ...it's great... collaborative group work really works, they loved it, they got so involved they didn't want to go out at break.

They also analysed the materials in terms of their success in providing EESF, which helped them to rework their understanding of the theory which underpinned the CCW document and the planning framework which they had used to inform their writing:

...you could see them developing their understanding of the relationship between the natural world and how human beings use it, you know the social and the natural, like we discussed.

...the role plays gave the children the chance to rehearse a range of viewpoints and, in role, attempt to persuade others to their point of view.

...they practised political action, mine invited their MP to come and watch their simulation of the 1995 Ocean Summit.

...now I've tried it I can see the value of active learning, it really helps the children clarify their values and makes them want to take responsibility for environmental action.

...I liked the way the materials gave children the knowledge they needed to understand the environmental problems, and how complex they are.

...it didn't depress them though I thought it would, instead it seemed to empower them.

They also reflected on the potentially controversial nature of the materials, and the importance of giving the children a critical perspective so as to avoid indoctrination:

I thought my teacher would be worried that I was indoctrinating the children, but because they were working out for themselves what the problems were and seeing that different people had different ideas about solutions it was OK.

I can see now why you (the tutor) called it critical education, because the children were dealing with the causes of the problems and how they might be solved, not just finding out what the problems were.

Yeah, like they wanted to know who decides, and how do the people making the decisions think about the future. These are all critical questions.

It seems that what they were doing was learning how to think critically and understand what they could do about environmental issues in a democracy.

Conclusion

This work took students on a journey of investigation and interrogation of the discourse of environmental education. The classroom materials they developed arose out of the meaning they ascribed to that discourse, meanings which were both personal and shared. This process has a wider value as it also challenges the view which is currently gaining currency, of teaching as a set of technical skills and teachers as technicians who must accept the goals and values of the National Curriculum without question.

Perhaps the students who were involved in this project will become teachers who have the competence and ability to achieve the goal of EESF. Students were aware of the possibilities and constraints of the National Curriculum, and of the schools and classrooms in which they worked, and attempted to achieve a match between the rhetoric and the practice. In this sense the materials were developed through a principled process which sets them apart from most materials prepared for teachers.

The two projects described above provide examples which other teacher educators may like to draw on in their own course planning and development. They were characterised by a commitment to real-life issues which required students to engage in group-based curriculum development and critical evaluation. This reflective model of teacher education challenges the technician model of teaching which seems set to dominate teacher education in Britain in the foreseeable future. The work of the students also demonstrates that a holistic approach to the curriculum can both challenge the government's information-acquisition model and meet its demands. *Ocean Environments* (Lyle et al, 1994) covers much of the statutory content of the National Curriculum, and the processes and methods of teaching which it uses and promotes also ensure that children are introduced to a critical enquiry approach to learning.

EESF requires the education of critical thinkers. The work discussed here provided a context for student teachers to engage in systematic reflection on their own practice. The process in which they participated involved:

☐ collaboration to develop a critical understanding of EESF;

☐ applying this understanding to the planning of classroom

☐ materials which meet curriculum requirements;

☐ using the materials in school, thus deepening their understanding of learning and teaching and its relationship to EESF;

☐ systematically reflecting on the materials in order to improve them.

By looking critically and systematically at their materials, after they had been used in the classroom, they increased their understanding of wider educational issues. They became developers of curriculum, not mere implementors. Such practice provides student teachers with many of the skills we associate with action research.

This work was carried out as a voluntary project run in the students' and tutor's own time. It enabled students to see themselves as critically reflective educators. Will the new agenda for teacher education mean that such work becomes less and less possible? Teachers at all stages of their professional development need the opportunity to reflect systematically on their pedagogical practices, which is important if the values and concerns of global education is to flourish in the schools and classrooms of a democratic society.

CHAPTER 17

The Inner Self and Becoming a Teacher

Veronica Voiels

This is myself within my heart.
Smaller than a grain of rice or a
barley corn or a mustard seed or the
kernel of grain of millet. This is my
Self within my heart, greater than
the earth, greater than the
atmosphere, greater than all these
worlds. All works, all desires, all
scents, all tastes belong to it: it
encompasses all this universe
(*Chandogya Upanishad*, Book 3,
chapter xiv, verses 4-5).

Introduction

The relationship between the inner
personal world of the teacher and the
outer world of global education is the
focus for this chapter. My proposition is
that the process of self-analysis and
reflection upon the values, concerns
and experiences which are essential to
human development is a necessary
precondition for a mature and genuine
response to moral, cultural and global
issues in the classroom. In my teaching
in Religious Education with both
postgraduate and BEd students at
Manchester Metropolitan University, I

have attempted to incorporate
opportunities for engaging in this
process of exploring the inner self, as
well as providing a global dimension to
the subject and the methodologies of
teacher education. In this chapter I will
be discussing the theoretical basis for
this approach to professional
development, the place of global
education within my work in initial
teacher training, and an evaluation of
the approaches used.

The concept of the inner self

Educational theory has been
fundamentally influenced by a range of
psychological theories which stress the
importance of engaging with the inner
self as a resource for personal growth
and professional development (Mead,
1935; Jung, 1958; Rogers, 1969; Hirst
and Peters, 1970; Burns, 1982).

In the symbolic interactionist schools
of social psychology, the discovery of
the self is an essential part of the
process of personal development. Mead
describes the evolution of the concept of
the self through the process of

internalisation of expected norms from 'significant others' (Mead, 1935). Jungian theory locates the true self at the point of integration between the realms of the unconscious and conscious minds (Jung, 1958). Within the religious and spiritual frame of reference, the realisation of the nature of the inner self involves a belief in a soul or inner spirit, ie non-physical dimension to human nature. While this spiritual understanding of the self would not be accepted by all teachers, some educationalists assert that a recognition and exploration of the inner self has its role to play in the process of becoming a teacher.

Whereas psychology is no longer an important element in teacher education in Britain, elsewhere it has a more central role, as these examples from Denmark and Canada illustrate:

> In the schools there ought to be teaching of inner development, of balancing personality. Our society, our very times, are one-sidedly extrovert.... The education of teachers ought to give a higher priority to personal development... The work as a teacher demands that one involves oneself emotionally and personally, therefore problems of an emotional and personal nature must of course be included. The educator must work with his or her own personality and have the audacity to use it as a tool in the teaching (Kragh, 1993).

Self-awareness is seen as a source of strength and security in a teacher's professional work.

Working with Canadian teachers, Hunt has developed a range of strategies which assist teachers in 'bringing out experienced knowledge' ie. 'our accumulated understanding of human affairs which resides in our hearts, heads and actions', an 'untapped resource waiting to be discovered and brought out' (Hunt 1991). Using methodologies such as guided meditation and journalling, teachers were able to recall significant and positive professional experiences and reflect upon them to identify self-perceptions, implicit theories and personal images. These implicit theories are ' the underlying beliefs we hold about the nature of human affairs'.

They relate to:

☐ perceptions or the dimensions of considering others;

☐ intentions or hopes and goals in working with others;

☐ the ways in which they work towards achieving their goals.

Teachers can discover their underlying beliefs about their role, such as 'as a guide through life', ' an instructor' or 'a fellow learner' or a 'facilitator'. This sensitive awareness of their inner selves enabled Hunt's teachers to become more confident and aware of their own inner resources and use them more consciously and creatively in teaching. His work starts from a psychological base and demonstrates the links between the teacher's inner psychology and their professional priorities. My own approach to teacher education has been shaped by the same aim of helping students connect with their inner wisdom and experienced knowledge in order to become good teachers.

On becoming an RE teacher

One of the most commonly stated hopes of students embarking on a course of initial teacher training is ' to stand in front of the class and keep control'. As an HE tutor my aim is to extend this pragmatic need for a survival kit into the more valuable processes of personal and professional development. Becoming a teacher involves a variety of skills and experiences ranging from the inner reserves of confidence, sensitivity and faith in human nature, to the more intellectual and communication skills in preparing and delivering the curriculum.

The current political climate within teacher education has led to a range of competing models. Diamond (1991) highlights some of the tensions and dilemmas faced by those teacher educators who seek to preserve 'Personalistic Teacher Education'

He argues that in PTE:

> teachers each develop in a unique way and that to be educated they must be able to formulate adequate selves, personal agendas and keen appreciations of the needs of others... Its underlying epistemological foundations are broadly phenomenological and rely heavily on perceptual and developmental psychology (Diamond, 1991).

In contrast, Competency Based Teacher Education (CBTE) is the model that was preferred by the Council of Accreditation for Teacher Education (CATE) and presently by the Teacher Training Agency (TTA). This approach is based on prior specification of competences that teachers should acquire in order to perform certain tasks, and undermines the importance of teachers as 'uniquely intentional persons' and the exploration of the inner self in the process of becoming a teacher.

However, in my work in Religious Education it is precisely the process of exploring the inner self which is an essential aspect in preparing student teachers to deal with the moral, cultural and global issues which naturally arise in their work. By focusing on the spiritual and moral dimensions of the curriculum, students need to reflect upon what this means for themselves and for their role and responsibility as an educator of children and young people growing up at this time.

The changing nature of RE reflects the changing nature of British society, as Enwin Cox (1989) points out in his comparison of the legal requirements for RE in the 1944 and 1988 Education Acts. Whereas the former was written during World War Two when national loyalty and identity were required, the second was conceived in a pluralistic and multi-ethnic society. The debates in RE about the extent to which it should reflect the cultural heritage of Britain or take account of the pluralistic multi-faith nature of modern Britain and of global society, mirror the wider debates about the nature and purpose of education in our schools today.

The model RE syllabuses recently published by SCM (1994) to guide local authorities in their development of locally agreed syllabuses have responded to this debate in a balanced way. Whilst these guidelines entail Christianity being taught at each key stage, they also insist that all pupils are entitled to learn about — and from — each of the major religious traditions of the world. This does allow the teacher to help children appreciate the pluralistic nature of British society and of the world. Furthermore, these models stress the development of attitudes in religious education such as commitment, fairness, respect, self-understanding and enquiry. Additionally the legal requirement that the curriculum is 'balanced and broadly based and promotes the spiritual, moral, mental and physical development of pupils' (ERA 1988) focuses discussion on the nature of spiritual and moral development. This was highlighted in a recent Ofsted discussion paper:

> This publication is unashamedly about values. Above all it reflects the fact that successive pieces of educational legislation have had at their centre their belief that education in this country is not only about the gaining of knowledge and the acquiring of essential skills ... but also about personal development in its fullest sense (Ofsted, 1994).

It can be argued that this focus on personal values has always been a central concern of RE. The importance of our own personal histories and subjective experience in the process of becoming a teacher is fully explored by Grimmett, whose work relates religious education to the humanistic psychology and personalistic teacher education discussed above:

> Our subjectivity incorporates what might be called personal vision and although this is subject to change, it provides us with a continuing filter

for our cognitive, affective, and spiritual experiences (Grimmett, 1987).

Throughout this century, moral philosophers have strongly asserted that the development of a personal value system should not take place within a narrowly conceived cultural context. Piaget (1932), Dewey (1935) and Kohlberg (1980), amongst others, highlight the impact that living in a pluralistic society makes upon the moral development of the individual:

> All of their accounts assume that the developed person can draw from the diverse treasures of particular cultures without being caught in the web of any one cultures' traditional authority and norms (Power and Power, 1992).

Becoming a global teacher

The central aim of world studies is 'to develop the knowledge, attitudes and skills which young people need in order to practise social and environmental responsibility in a multicultural society and interdependent world' (Hicks and Steiner, 1989). This central aim has an obvious affinity with the aims of RE. Richardson (1982) proposes seven principles within the humanities curriculum that underpin the appropriate skills and attitudes young people need to understand 'other' cultures. I have transposed these into the context of Religious Education.

☐ Students need to acknowledge the variety and differences within a faith and never assume that 'all Muslims, Sikhs, Hindus et cetera are.'

□ Students should perceive followers of different faiths as human beings similar to themselves, with hopes, anxieties, will-power et cetera.

□ Student should see 'other' faiths as morally virtuous and not evil.

□ Students should be given the chance to interact with other faiths.

□ Students should appreciate the interdependence of cultures.

□ Students should recognise the causes and origin of stereotyping religious traditions as well as the dangers of it.

□ Students should explore the concept of justice through the study of religion.

There is a clear affinity in terms of moral development and cultural understanding between RE and global education (see, *inter alia*, Fisher and Hicks, 1985; Pike and Selby, 1988; Steiner, 1993). Over the past decade, I have sought to integrate the world studies framework of concepts, skills, attitudes, teaching methodologies and resources directly into my teaching. Working in partnership with colleagues in development education and world studies on university courses in global education and religious education has revitalised some of my initial approaches and extended the range of teaching methodologies I now use.

Putting it into practice

RE has to take into account the wider issues of justice, equality, respect for the rights of the individual and diversity in society, as well as a more explicit focus on the role of values in education in relation to the basic purpose of education and specifically in RE. I encourage the students to look beyond the information and consider why it is important to know and understand about world religions and how this knowledge relates to issues of cultural identity, diversity, human rights and global concerns.

Yet a 'global teacher' must go beyond these intellectual levels of understanding. My relationship as a HE tutor with student teachers and trainees is consciously based on the principles which underpin global education in the classroom. These ensure that the values of affirmation, co-operation, mutual respect and interdependence determine how we relate to each other as teachers and learners. In organising sessions for PGCE and BEd students, careful attention is given to the dynamics in the group in order to nurture and develop these qualities, so that students experience for themselves how central these are to the learning process.

These values and principles are also modelled in the student-centred learning incorporated into my classes by using experiential activities more extensively, especially creative visualisation. This method effectively combines experience of looking inwards while giving scope and space to imagine and relate to the wider global world. (See Hay, 1989; Hammond et al, 1990; Burns and Lamont, 1993)

In the courses on subject applications with first and third year BEd students, I have established that it is essential to good RE teaching to value the richness of personal experience and treat it as an integral part of the learning process. For example, when using artefacts or photographs of religious symbols or sacred places, to reflect upon the places and objects sacred to oneself in order to appreciate how these can have meaning and importance to others. I have developed and evaluated this approach more systematically elsewhere (Voiels, 1994).

Students' perspectives

To give value and importance to self-awareness and personal experience in learning, allow time for reflection and evaluation of the learning process in a variety of ways. For example, when evaluating a session students might consider:

☐ What effect has this session had on your self-understanding?

☐ What effect has this session had on your understanding of being a teacher?

☐ How has it affected your values, priorities and attitudes as a teacher?

☐ What values and issues for you as a person and as a teacher were raised by this particular session?

Their very positive feedback clearly indicates that such commonly shared values in education benefit teachers and learners:

These sessions also broadened my own knowledge of the world and our place in it and the issues involved, not least from the other students on the course who also brought with them a wealth of knowledge and ideas which I gained much from.

This option has been rewarding in may ways. On a personal level the course has forced me to focus inwards and look at myself as a spiritual being and as such my relationship to the rest of the world. On a professional level the course has provided me with some stimulating ideas on teaching my main subject, English.

This course has not only made a valuable contribution to my subject teaching but also to developing a more positive relationship with my pupils.

World studies challenges the individual to think about oneself and how one interacts on a wider basis in the world around us. In my professional life I see many opportunities to become involved and facilitate such activities. As an RE specialist the basic values of world studies such as 'similarities and differences' and 'values and beliefs' fit naturally into an RE curriculum.

The students' evaluations reveal that the principles and practices of global education provide valuable opportunities for personal and professional growth. The relationship between personal values and professional commitment as an area of experience is a core focus in Religious Education and global education. Students and practising teachers soon realise that the reason they are attracted to such work is the possibility of exploring and utilising their inner selves, their personal values and priorities for the wider purpose of becoming a better teacher. This in its turn contributes to better relationships between teachers and learners, based on mutual respect and trust. The Ofsted inspection of the School of Education at Manchester Metropolitan University in 1994/5 acknowledged the positive commitment of the staff to the professional development of students as shown by the exemplary models of the teacher role in college sessions and the excellent relationships between tutors, students and mentors in school.

The need to keep developing such courses goes beyond the pragmatic concern for effective management of groups and classes. It provides a positive and affirming context for the student teacher to discover their own guiding principles. With pressures to increase the size of groups and fragment the process of teacher education relationships between HE tutors and students are seriously threatened. Furthermore, the continuing efforts to impose principles and practices of the market economy into institutions of education produce conflicts of interest which undermine the principles of affirmation, co-operation, respect and openmindedness characteristic of global education. It is all the more important in teacher education to maintain these principles and make possible the experience of a harmonious and caring environment in which learning can take place.

References

References for Introduction

Apple, M. (1993) *Official Knowledge: Democratic Education in a Conservative Age*, London: Routledge.

Dahrendorff, R. (1990) 'The Coming Decade of Citizenship', London: *The Guardian*, August 1, 1990.

Falk, R. (1994) 'The Making of Global Citizenship' in van Steenbergen, B. (Ed.) *The Condition of Citizenship*, London: Sage Publications p.131.

Heater, D. (1990) *Citizenship: The Civic Ideal in World History, Politics and Education*, London: Longman.

hooks, b. (1994) *Teaching to Transgress: Education as the Practice of Freedom*, London: Routledge.

Huckle, J. (1996) 'Globalisation, Postmodernity and Citizenship' in Steiner, M. (ed.) *Developing the Global Teacher: Theory and Practice in Teacher Education*, Stoke-on-Trent: Trentham Books.

Kirkpatrick, E. M. (1983) (Ed.) *Chambers Twentieth Century Dictionary*, Edinburgh: W. and R. Chambers Ltd.

Lynch, J. (1992) *Education for Citizenship in a Multicultural Society*, London, Cassell p.2-3.

Marshall, T. H. (1950) *Citizenship and Social Class,* Cambridge: Cambridge University Press.

National Curriculum Council (1990) *Curriculum Guidance 8: Education for Citizenship,* York: NCC p.15.

Osler, A. (1994) *Development Education: Global Perspectives in the Curriculum,* London: Cassell.

Richardson, R. (1979) 'Education for Change' in Thomas, O. (Ed.). *The Third World in Initial Teacher Training*, Oxford: Oxfam Education.

Richardson, R. (1995) 'National Identity: Debates and Musings in Britain, Summer 1995', *The Runnymede Bulletin* ,288 September 1995.

Roberts, A. (*Daily Mail*, 1995) quoted in Moore, S. 'Flying the Flag of Convenience', London: *The Guardian*, July 20, 1995.

Steiner, M. Moscovitch and Voiels, V. (1995) *Preparing to Teach for Citizenship,* Seminar Paper presented to Erasmus Action *Learning democracy, social justice, global responsibility and respect for human rights*, Berlin.

Tate, N. (1995), 'Friends, subjects and citizens', London: *The Guardian*, September 5, 1995.

Thomas, O. (Ed.) (1979) *The Third World in Initial Teacher Training*, Oxford: Oxfam Education.

References for Chapter 1

Camus, A. (1940) article in *The Adelphi Magazine*, April-June 1940, quoted in Henderson, James L. (1963) *World Questions: a study guide*, London: Methuen, p.238.

Henderson, James L. (1968) *Education for World Understanding*, Oxford: Pergamon, p.85.

Runnymede Trust (1992) *Equality Assurance in Schools: quality, identity, society*, Stoke-on-Trent: Trentham Books.

References for Chapter 3

Apple, M. in Liston, D. and Zeichner, K. (1991) *Teacher Education and the Social Conditions of Schooling*, London: Routledge.

Brown, M. (1996) *Teaching and Learning Styles: Materials for Staff Development*, Oldham: TVEI, Oldham.

Campbell, B and Davies, I. (1995) 'Education and Green Citizenship: An Exploratory Study with Student Teachers', *Research Papers in Educational Studies 95/01,* University of York.

Department for Education (1993) *The Initial Training of Primary School Teachers: New Criteria for Course Approval (Circular 14/93),* London: DFE.

Fisher, S. and Hicks,D.(1985) *World Studies 8-13: A Teacher's Handbook,* Edinburgh: Oliver and Boyd p.15.

Gardiner, H. (1993) *The Unschooled Mind,* London: Fontana p.250.

Giroux, H. (1989) *Schooling for Democracy: Critical Pedagogy in the Modern Age,* London: Routledge.

Giroux, H. (1992) *Border Crossings,* London: Routledge.

Hicks, D (Ed.) (1994) *Preparing for the Future,* London: Adamantine Press p.11.

Hicks, D. and Holden, C. (1995) *Visions of the Future,* Stoke-on-Trent: Trentham Books.

hooks, b (1993) 'Transformative Pedagogy and Multiculturalism' in *Freedom's Plough,* Perry, T. and Fraser, J. (Eds), London: Routledge.

hooks, b. (1994) *Teaching to Transgress,* London: Routledge pp.14-15, 19.

Huckle, J. (1989) 'Lessons from political education' in Hicks, D. and Steiner, M. (Eds.) *Making Global Connections,* Edinburgh: Oliver and Boyd.

Huckle, J. (1992) quoted in Fien, J. (1992) *Education for the Environment: Critical Curriculum Theorising and Environmental Education,* Victoria: Deakin University Press p.39.

Huckle, J. et al (1995) *Reaching Out: Education for Sustainability,* Godalming: World Wide Fund for Nature.

Klein, G. (1994) 'Equal Rights in the Classroom?' The role of teacher education in ensuring equality of educational opportunities, *Educational Review,* 46(2), pp.167-177.

Lipman, M., (1991) *Thinking in Education,* Cambridge: Cambridge University Press.

Manchester Metropolitan University (1995) *PGCE Secondary One Year Course 1994-1995, Course Handbook,* Manchester: MMU p.78.

Martin, J. R. (1987) *Reclaiming a conversation: The ideal of the educated woman*: 406, New Haven:

Yale University Press in Liston, D. and Zeichner, K. (1991).

Miller, J. Baker (1976) *Toward a New Psychology of Women,* Harmondsworth: Penguin p.5.

Pike, G. and Selby, D. (1988) *Global Teacher, Global Learner,* London: Hodder and Stoughton.

Richardson, R. (1979) *Learning for Change,* London: World Studies Project.

Richardson, R. (1990) *Daring to be a Teacher,* Stoke-on-Trent: Trentham Books pp.42-43.

Siraj-Blatchford, I. (1993) 'Social Justice and Teacher Education in the UK' in Verma, G. K. (Ed.) *Inequality and Teacher Education,* London: Falmer Press.

Steiner, M. (1993) *Learning from Experience,* Stoke-on-Trent: Trentham Books.

Steiner, M. Moscovitch and Voiels, V. (1995) *Preparing to Teach for Citizenship,* Seminar Paper presented to Erasmus Action 'Learning democracy, social justice, global responsibility and respect for human rights': Berlin.

Tough, A. (1991) *Critical Questions About the Future,* London: Adamantine Press p.51.

Verma, G. K. 'Teacher Education and Inequality' in Verma, G. K. (Ed.), *Inequality and Teacher Education,* London: Falmer Press.

Weiler, K.,(1991) 'Freire and a Feminist Pedagogy of Difference' *Harvard Educational Review* 61(4), pp.449-474.

Weiner, G. (1994) *Feminisms in Education,* Buckingham: The Open University Press p.125.

Whitaker, P. (1995) *Managing to Learn,* London: Cassell p.55.

References for Chapter 4

Allen, J. (1992) 'Post-industrialism and Post-Fordism', in Hall, S.; Held, D. and McGrew, T. (eds.), op.cit.

Barnaby, F. (ed.) (1988) *The Gaia Peace Atlas,* London: Pan Books.

Beck, U. (1992) *Risk Society: Towards a New Modernity,* London: Sage.

Ekins, P. (1992) *Wealth Beyond Measure: an atlas of the new economics,* London: Gaia Books.

Ellwood, W. (1993) 'The new globalism', *The New Internationalist,* June.

Giddens, A. (1991) *Modernity and Self Identity: Self and Society in the Late Modern Age*, Oxford: Polity.

Gilbert, R. (1992) 'Citizenship, Education and Postmodernity', British Journal of Sociology of Education, 13/1.

Gilbert, R. (1995) 'Education for Citizenship and the Problem of Identity in Post-modern Political Culture' in Ahier, J. and Ross, A. (eds.) *The Social Subjects within the Curriculum: Children's social learning in the National Curriculum,* London: Falmer, (passim and 20).

Giroux, H. (1992) *Border Crossings: Cultural Workers and the Politics of Education*, London: Routledge.

Hall, S; Held, D. and McGrew, T. (eds.) (1992) *Modernity and its Futures*, Cambridge: Open University/Polity.

Harvey, D. (1989) The Condition of Postmodernity, Oxford: Blackwell.

Held, D. (1994a) 'What Should Democracy Mean Today?' in *The Polity Reader in Social Theory,* Cambridge: Polity Press, (passim and 311).

Held, D. (1994b) 'Democracy: From City-states to a Cosmopolitan Order?' in *The Polity Reader in Social Theory*, Cambridge: Polity Press.

Hill, D. (1991) 'What's Left in Teacher Education: Teacher Education the Radical Left and Policy Proposals for the 1990s', in Chitty, C. (ed.) *Changing the Future: Redprint for Education,* London: Tufnell Press.

Huckle, J. (1988) *What We Consume: the Teachers Handbook*, Richmond: Richmond Publishing Company/WWF-UK.

Huckle, J. (1993) *Our Consumer Society* (Unit 3 of *What We Consume*), Richmond: Richmond Publishing Company/WWF-UK.

IUCN/UNEP/WWF, (1991) *Caring for the Earth: A Strategy for Sustainable Living*, Gland.

Lash, S. and Urry, J. (1994) *Economies of Signs and Space*, London: Sage.

Lynch, J. (1992) *Education for Citizenship in a Multicultural Society*, London: Cassell.

McGrew, T. (1992) 'A Global Society?' in Hall, S. Held, D. and McGrew, T. (eds.), op.cit.

Oliver, D. and Heater, D. (1994) *The Foundations of Citizenship*, Hemel Hempstead: Harvester Wheatsheaf.

Segal, G. (1993) *The World Affairs Companion,* London: Simon and Schuster.

Smart, B. (1993) *Postmodernity*, London: Routledge.

Swift, A. (1993) *Global Political Ecology: the Crisis in Economy and Government*, London: Pluto.

Usher, R. and Edwards, R. (1994) *Postmodernism and Education*, London: Routledge, (passim and 214).

Wainwright, H. (1994) *Arguments for a New Left, Answering the Free-Market Right*, Oxford: Blackwell.

Zeichner, K. M. (1993) 'Connecting Genuine Teacher Development to the Struggle for Social Justice', *Journal of Education for Teaching*, 19/1, 5-20.

References for Chapter 5

Barrett, E. et al (1992) *Initial Teacher Education in England and Wales: A Topography*, London: Goldsmiths College.

Furlong, J. (1992) The limits of competence: a cautionary note on Circular 9/92. Unpublished paper: University of Swansea.

Giroux, H. (1988) *Schooling and the Struggle for Public Life*, Minneapolis: University of Minnesota.

Hicks, D. (1994) *Educating for the Future: A Practical Classroom Guide*, Godalming: WWF.

HMI (1994) *Draft Working Papers for the Inspection of Primary Initial Teacher Training.*

Kimber, D. et al (1995) *Humanities in Primary Education*, London: David Fulton.

Lynch, J. (1992) *Education for Citizenship in a Multicultural Society*: London, Cassell.

Menter, I. and Clough, N. (1995) Towards a philosophy and pedagogy for democratic citizenship in a new Europe: some lessons from Latvia, in Tsch'oumy, J. A. ed. *Le Choc de la Democratie*, Lyon: ATEE.

Schon, D. (1983) *The Reflective Practitioner*, New York: Basic Books.

Schon, D. (1987) *Educating the Reflective Practitioner*, San Francisco, Jossey Bass.

Whitty, G. and Willmott, E. (1991) Competence based teacher education: approaches and issues, *Cambridge Journal of Education*, 21, 3, 309-3.

Zeichner, K. (1982) Reflective teaching and field based experience in pre-service teacher education, *Interchange*, 12.

References for Chapter 6

African National Congress (1993) *A Policy Framework for Education and Training,* Johannesburg: ANC.

Andrews, R. (1994) *International Dimensions of the National Curriculum,* Stoke-on-Trent: Trentham Books.

Channer, Y. (1995) *I am a Promise,* Stoke-on-Trent: Trentham Books.

Commission for Race Equality (1988) *Ethnic Minority Schoolteachers,* London: CRE.

Fisher, S. and Hicks, D. (1983) *World Studies 8-13* Edinburgh: Oliver and Boyd.

Grunsell, A. and Wade, R. (1995) 'Where do we go from here?' *Multicultural Teaching* 13.3.

Hicks, D. and Steiner, M.(1989) *Making Global Connections,* Edinburgh: Oliver and Boyd.

King, A. and Reiss, M. (eds.) (1993) *The Multicultural Dimension of the National Curriculum,* Lewes: Falmer.

Klein, G. (1993) *Education towards Race Equality,* London: Cassell.

Klein, G. (1994) 'Equal rights in the classroom? The role of teacher education in ensuring equality of educational opportunities', *Educational Review,* 46.2.

Massey, I. (1995) 'Education against racism and xenophobia in Europe', *Multicultural Teaching,* 14.1.

Macdonald, I. et.al (1989) *Murder in the Playground,* London: Longsight Press.

Nehaul, K. (1996) *The Schooling of Children of Caribbean Heritage,* Stoke-on-Trent: Trentham Books.

Richardson, R. (1996) *Fortunes and Fables: Education for hope in troubled times,* Stoke-on-Trent: Trentham Books.

Robbins, M. Moyo (1995) 'Black students in teacher education', *Multicultural Teaching.* 14.1.

Runnymede Trust (1993) *Equality Assurance in Schools,* Stoke-on-Trent: Trentham Books.

Siraj-Blatchford, I. (1990) 'Positive discrimination: the underachievement of initial teacher education', *Multicultural Teaching,* 8.2.

Showunmi, V. and Constantine-Simms, D. (eds.) (1995) *Teachers for the Future,* Stoke-on-Trent: Trentham Books.

Steiner, M. (1993 *Learning from Experience: World Studies in the primary classroom,* Stoke-on-Trent: Trentham Books with World Studies Trust.

Troyna, B. and Carrington, B. (1990) *Education, Racism and Reform,* London: Routledge.

Troyna, B. and Hatcher, R. (1992) *Racism in Children's Lives,* London: Routledge.

References for Chapter 7

Andrews, R. (1994) *International Dimensions in the National Curriculum,* Stoke-on-Trent: Trentham Books p.viii.

Anti-Racist Teacher Education Network (1988) 'Permeation: the Road to Nowhere', *Occasional Paper no 4,* Glasgow: Jordan Hill College of Education.

Commission for Racial Equality (1987) *Learning in Terror,* London: Commission for Racial Equality.

Fogelman, K. (ed) (1991) *Citizenship in Schools,* London: David Fulton publishers.

Great Britain, Department for Education and Science (1981) *West Indian Children in Our Schools* (the Rampton Report), London: Her Majesty's Stationery Office.

Great Britain, Department for Education and Science (1985) *Education for All* (the Swann Report), London: Her Majesty's Stationery Office.

Gillborn, D. (1990) *Race, Ethnicity and Education,* London: Unwin Hyman.

Gundara, J., Jones, C. and Kimberley, K (eds) (1986) *Racism, Diversity and Education,* London: Hodder and Stoughton.

Klein, G. (1993), *Education Towards Race Equality,* London: Cassell

Lynch, J. (1992) *Education for Citizenship in a Multicultural Society,* London and New York, London: Cassell.

Modgil, S., Verma, G., Mallick, K. and Modgil, C. (eds) (1986) *Multicultural Education: the Interminable Debate,* East Sussex, UK and Bristol, USA: the Falmer Press.

Myers, K. (ed) (1992) *Genderwatch! After the Education Reform Act,* Cambridge: Cambridge University Press.

National Curriculum Council (1990) *Curriculum Guidance no 8: Education for Citizenship,* London: National Curriculum Council.

The Report of the South Commission (1990) *The Challenge to the South*, Oxford: Oxford University Press.

Rogers, P., 'International Citizenship', in Fogelman, K. (ed) (1991) *Citizenship in Schools*, London: David Fulton Publishers.

Runnymede Trust (1993) *Equality Assurance in Schools: Quality, Identity, Society: A Handbook for Action Planning and School Effectiveness*, Stoke-on-Trent: Trentham Books.

Shah, S. (1989) 'Effective Permeation of Race and Gender Issues in Teacher Education Courses' in *Gender and Education,* vol 1 no 3 pp.221-236.

Shah, S. (1991) The Changing Role of the Tutor in S. Shah, S. (ed) *Learner Managed Learning: The Power to Learn*, London: Institute of Education, for World Education Fellowship.

Sheffield City Polytechnic (1991) Gender and Teacher Education Conference: *Working Papers and Workshop Materials*: Sheffield.

World Commission on Environment and Development (1987) *Our Common Future* (Brundtland Report), Oxford and New York: Oxford University Press.

References Chapter 8

CAFOD et al, (1990) *Questioning Fundraising*: London.

Lamont, G. and Burns, S. (1993) *Values and Visions: Initial Guidelines*, Manchester: Development Education Project.

References for Chapter 9

Bovey, M. (1991) *Values, Cultures and Kids*, London: Stanley Thornes.

Epstein, D. (1993) *Changing Classroom Cultures: Anti-Racism, Politics and Schools*, Stoke-on-Trent: Trentham Books.

Featherstone, M. (Ed) (1990) *Global Culture: Nationalism, Globalisation, Identity*, London: Sage.

Gates, H. L. (1994) *Coloured People: A memoir*, New York: Knopf.

Grosvenor, I. (1990) Education, Racism and the Employment of Black Teachers, *Multicultural Teaching* 8(2) pp.9-13.

Institute of Race Relations (IRR) (1994) *Outcast England: How Schools Exclude Black Children*, London: IRR.

Lynch, J (1992) *Education for Citizenship in a Multicultural Society*, London: Cassell.

Meighan, R and J., and Harber, C. (1989) Democratic Practice: Missing Item on the Agenda of Teacher Education, in Harber, C. and Meighan, R. (Eds) *The Democratic School. Educational Management and the Practice of Democracy*, Ticknall: Education Now Books.

Menter, I. and Braunholtz, R. (1990) Anti-Racism: Teaching and professionalism, *Multicultural Teaching* 9(3) pp.8-11.

Menter, I. (1992) The New Right, Racism and Teacher Education; Some Recent Developments, *Multicultural Teaching* 10(2) pp.6-9.

Modood, T. (1992) *Not Easy Being British: Colour, Culture and Citizenship*, London: Runnymede Trust in association with Trentham Books, Stoke-on-Trent.

Mumma, O. (1993) Drama and Education as Contesting Cultures: Historical Perspectives in Kenya, *SCYPT Journal* (Standing Committee on Young Peoples' Theatre) 26 pp.41-47.

Osler, A. (Ed) (1994) *Development Education: Global Perspectives in the Curriculum*, London: Cassell.

Rabinow, P. (Ed) (1984) *The Foucault Reader: An Introduction to Foucault's Thought*, London: Penguin.

Richardson, R. (1992) Introduction in Modood, T. *Not Easy Being British: Colour, Culture and Citizenship*, London: Runnymede Trust in association with Trentham Books, Stoke-on-Trent.

Roberts, H.R., Gonzalez, J.C., Harris, O. D., Huff, D., Lou, R. and Scott, O. (1994) *Teaching in the Multicultural Classroom*, London: Sage.

Solomos, J. and Back, L. (1995) *Race, Politics and Social Change*, London: Routledge.

Taylor, B. (1986) Anti-Racist Education in Non-Contact Areas: The Need for a Gentle Approach, *New Community* 13(2) pp.177-184.

Taylor, B. (1987) Anti-Racist Education in Predominantly White Areas, *Journal of Further and Higher Education* 11(3), pp.45-48.

Tomlinson, S. (1990) *Multicultural Education in White Schools*, London: Batsford.

References for Chapter 10

Baddersley, P. and Eddershaw, C. (1994) *Not so Simple Picture Books*, Stoke-on-Trent: Trentham Books.

Baron, J.B. and Sternberg, R.J. (eds) *Teaching Thinking Skills*, New York: Freeman.

Birmingham Development Education Centre (1991) *Start with a Story*, Birmingham: DEC.

Birmingham Development Education Centre (1994) *Long Ago and Far Away*, Birmingham: DEC.

Bruner, J. (1987) *Making Sense — a child's construction of the world*, Methuen: London.

Cam, P. ed. (1993) *Thinking Stories 1*, Book and Resource Book, Sydney, Australia: Hale and Iremonger.

Coles, M.J. and Robinson, W. (1991) *Teaching Thinking*, London: Bristol Classical Press (2nd.edition).

De Hamel (1985) *Hemi's Pet*, North Ryde, NSW, Australia: Angus and Robertson.

Dewey, J. (1963) *Experience and Education*, London: Collier- Macmillan.

Donaldson, M. (1993) *Human Minds*, Harmondsworth: Penguin.

Fisher, R. (1990), *Teaching Children to Think*, Oxford: Blackwell.

Freire, P. (1990), 'The Politics of Education' in Murphy P. and Moon B. (eds.) *Developments in Learning and Assessment*, Buckingham: Open University Press.

Lipman, M., Sharp, A. and Oscanyan F.S. (1980) *Philosophy in the Classroom*, Philadelphia: Temple University Press.

Lipman, M. and Sharpe, M. (1987) *Kio and Gus, Wondering at the World*, University of America Press.

Lipman, M. (1988) *Philosophy Goes to School*, Philadelphia: Temple University Press.

Lipman, M. (1991) *Thinking in Education,* Cambridge: Cambridge University Press.

Lipman, M. (1993) *Thinking Children and Education*, Dubuque, Iowa: Kendall/Hunt Publishing.

Murris, K. (1992) *Teaching Philosophy with Picture Books*: Infonet Publications.

Nattrass, J. (1994) Essay and Notes (unpublished), Charlotte Mason College, University of Lancaster.

Paul, R.W. (1991) *Critical Thinking; What Every Person Needs to Survive in a Rapidly Changing World*, Sonoma State University C.A., USA: Rohnert Park.

Rowe, D. (1994) *You, Me and Us*, London: Home Office.

Sharp, Ann M. (1990) 'What is a Community of Inquiry?' (unpublished), The Institute for the Advancement of Philosophy for Children, Montclair University, New Jersey.

Steiner, M (1993) *Learning From Experience*, Stoke-on-Trent: Trentham Books (pp.80-85).

Sprod, T. (1993) *Books into Ideas*, Hawker Brownlow.

Timson, J. (1995) 'Students rarely ask questions in classroom discussion: a triangulated study in search for reasons' (unpublished), Lancaster University, Dept. of Educational Research Small Scale Study.

Vygotsky, L. (1978) *Mind and Society*, Boston: Harvard University Press.

References for Chapter 11

Baines, L. (1992) *La Compôte Verte*, London: World Wide Fund for Nature.

Baines, L. (1992) *Das Grüne Kompott,* London: World Wide Fund for Nature.

Brown, K. and Brown, M. *The Changing World: a cross-curricular Modern Languages teaching pack*: forthcoming as part of the languages programme of the Centre for Global Education, University College of Ripon and York St. John.

Brown, M., D'Almeida, A., Stevenson, B. and Thorne C. *Teaching about francophone West Africa: Togo, a case study*: forthcoming as part of the languages programme of the Centre for Global Education, University College of Ripon and York St. John.

Byram, M. (1991) 'Background Studies' in English Foreign Language Teaching: lost opportunities in the Comprehensive School Debate, in Buttjes, D. and Byram, M. (eds) *Mediating Languages and Cultures: Towards an Intercultural Theory of Foreign Language Education*, Clevedon, England: Multilingual Matters Ltd.

Fisher, S. and Hicks, D. (1985) *World Studies 8-13 Handbook*, Edinburgh: Oliver and Boyd.

Mares, C. (1985) *Our Europe; Environmental Awareness and Language Development Through School Exchanges*, Brighton: Tidy Britain Group.

National Curriculum Council, (1990) *Curriculum Guidance 3, The Whole Curriculum,* York: National Curriculum Council.

Pike, G. and Selby, D. (1988) *Global Teacher, Global Learner*, London: Hodder and Stoughton.

Radnor, H. (1994) *Across the Curriculum*, London: Cassell.

Siraj-Blatchford, J. and I. (eds) (1995) *Educating the Whole Child: cross-curricular skills, themes and dimensions*, Buckingham: Open University Press.

Steiner, M. (1993) *Learning from Experience: co-operative learning and global education: A world studies source book*, Stoke-in-Trent: Trentham Books.

References for Chapter 12

Bowers, C.A. (1993) *Education, Cultural Myths, and the Ecological Crisis*, Albany: State University of New York Press.

Diamond, I. and Orenstein, G. (1990) *Reweaving the World: The Emergence of Ecofeminism*, San Francisco: Sierra Club Books.

Hicks, D. (1990) 'The World Studies 8-13 Project: a Short History 1980-89', *Westminster Studies in Education*, vol. 13, pp.61-80.

Hicks, D. (1994) *Educating for the Future: A Practical Classroom Guide*, Godalming: World Wide Fund for Nature UK.

Lister, I. (1987) 'Global and International Approaches in Political Education', in: Harber, C. ed. *Political Education in Britain*, Lewes: Falmer Press.

Litvinoff, M. (1990) *The Earthscan Action Handbook for People and Planet*, London: Earthscan Publications.

Orr, D. (1992) *Ecological Literacy: Education and the Transition to a Post-modern World*, Albany: State University of New York Press.

Orr, D. (1993) 'Schools for the Twenty-first Century', *Resurgence*, 160, September/October, pp.16-19.

Richardson, R. (1990) *Daring to be a Teacher: Essays, Stories and Memoranda*, Stoke-on-Trent: Trentham Books.

References to Chapter 13

Burr, M. (1992) *We Have Always Lived Here — The Maya of Guatemala*, London: Central America Human Rights Coordination.

Daniel P. and Bennell S. (1995) *Dod â Chanolbarth America i mewn i'r Cwricwlwm Cynradd/Bringing Central America into the Primary Curriculum*, (teachers' guide), Bangor: Grwp Canolbarth America Môn/Arfon Central America Group.

Daniel P. and Non Parri L. (1994) *Adlais o America Ladin/ Voices from Latin America/ Ecos de America Latina* (Trilingual poetry collection for use in schools), Bethesda: Grwp Canolbarth America Môn/Arfon Central America Group.

Development Education Centre (1995) *Development Compass Rose Consultation Pack*, Birmingham.

Renton, L. (1993) *The School is Us*, London: WWF UK with Manchester Development Education Project.

Sherston Software (1993) *Aztecs*, Malmesbury: Sherston Software Ltd.

References for Chapter 14

Brennan, F. et al (1994) *Guidelines for Good Practice in Development Education*, Dublin: DESC.

Freire, P. (1972) *Pedagogy of the Oppressed*, Hammondsworth: Penguin.

Hicks, D. and Townley, C. (eds) (1982) *Teaching World Studies*, Harlow: Longman.

Advisory Council on Development Co-operation (1985) *Development Education Report*, Dublin.

Osler, A. (ed) (1994) *Development Education: Global Perspectives in the Curriculum*, London: Cassell.

UNICEF, (1992) *Education for Development*, New York.

References for Chapter 15

Bale, J. (1987) *Geography in the Primary School*, London: Routledge and Kegan Paul.

Catling, S. (1993) 'The Whole World in Our Hands', *Geography* 78 (4) pp.340-58.

Cogan, J. (1982) Educating Teachers for a Global Perspective, *World Studies Journal* 4 (1) pp.20-23.

Commission on Geographical Education, International Geographer Union (IGU),

International Charter on Geographical Education, Brisbane: Queensland University of Technology.

DES (1991) *Geography in the National Curriculum,* London: HMSO.

Development Education Centre (1990) *Get the Picture,* Birmingham: Development Education Centre.

Fien, J. and Gerber, R. (eds) (1988) *Teaching Geography for a Better World,* Edinburgh: Oliver and Boyd.

Fountain, S. (1990) *Learning Together: Global Education 4-7,* Stanley Thornes Publishers Ltd with the World Wide Fund for Nature and the Centre for Global Education.

Fountain, S. (1995) *Education for Development: A Teacher's Resource for Global Learning,* London: Hodder and Stoughton.

Goodey, B. (1973) *Perception of the Environment: An Introduction to the Literature,* Occasional Paper No. 17, Birmingham: University of Birmingham Centre for Urban and Regional Studies.

HMI (1989) *Aspects of Primary Education: The Teaching and Learning of History and Geography,* London: HMSO.

Hicks, D. (1979) *Global Perspectives in the Curriculum: A Geographical Contribution,* Geography 64 (2) pp.104-14.

Hicks, D. (1994) *Preparing for the Future: Notes and Queries for Concerned Educators,* Adamantine Press p.26.

Hicks, D. and Steiner, M. (1989) *Making Global Connections,* Edinburgh: Oliver and Boyd.

Hopkin, J. (1994) 'Geography and Development Education' in Osler, A. (ed) *Development Education: Global Perspectives in the Curriculum,* London: Cassell.

Huckle, J. (ed) (1983) *Geographical Education: Reflection and Action,* Oxford University Press.

Lynch, J. (1992) *Education for Citizenship in a Multicultural Society,* London: Cassell.

McFarlane, C. (1986) *Hidden Messages? Activities for Exploring Bias,* Birmingham: Development Education Centre.

Ofsted (1993) *Geography Key Stages 1, 2 and 3, Second Year 1992- 1993,* London: HMSO.

Pike, G. and Selby, D. (1988) *Global Teacher, Global Learner,* London: Hodder and Stoughton.

Serf, J. and Sinclair, S. (eds) (1992) *Developing Geography,* Birmingham: Development Education Centre.

Steiner, M. (1993) *Learning from Experience: World Studies in the Primary Curriculum,* Stoke-on-Trent: Trentham Books with the World Studies Trust.

Wiegand, P. (1992) *Places in the Primary School: Knowledge and Understanding of Places at Key Stages 1 and 2,* Lewes: Falmer Press.

Wiegand, P. (1993) *Children and Primary Geography,* London: Cassell.

References for Chapter 16

Catholic Action For Overseas Development (1988) *Renewing the Earth — A Video,* London: CAFOD.

Council of Europe (1988) *Resolution of the Council and the Ministers of Education meeting with the Council, Environmental Education,* 88/C177/03: Council of Europe.

CCW (1992) *Advisory Paper 17: Environmental Education: A framework for Developing a Cross Curricular Theme in Wales,* p.14- 15, Cardiff: Curriculum Council for Wales.

DoE (1994) *Environmental Responsibility: An agenda for further and higher education,* p.9, London: HMSO.

DFE, (1993) *The Initial Training of Primary School Teachers: New Criteria for Course Approval* (Circular 14/93), London: DFE.

Fien, J. (1993) *Education for the Environment: A Pathway to Sustainability?,* Geelong: Deakin University Press.

IUCN/UNEP/WWF (1980) *World Conservation Strategy,* Nevada: IUCN UNEP WWF.

IUCN/UNEP/WWF (1991) *Caring for the Earth: A Strategy for Sustainable Development,* p.5, Nevada: IUCN/UNEP/WWF.

Lyle, S. and Halfacre, A. (1995) in Inman, S. (Ed) *Thinking Futures,* London: WWF/Richmond Publishers.

Lyle, S. and Hendley, D. (Eds) (1994) *Ocean Environments: A Geography/Science focused approach to Key Stage 2/3,* Swansea: Swansea Institute of Higher Education.

Sterling, S. (1990) 'Environment, Development and Education: Towards a Holistic View' in Lacey, C. and Williams, R. (1990) *Deception, Demonstration, Debate: Towards a Critical Education and*

Development Education, London: WWF (UK) and Kegan Paul.

UNESCO (1976) *The Belgrade Charter*, Paris: UNESCO.

UNESCO (1977) *Tbilisi Report*, Paris: UNESCO.

UNESCO-UNEP (1990) 'Environmental Education Teachers — the priority of priorities', *Connect* Vol. XV. No.1: UNESCO.

UNESCO, (1992) *UN Conference on Environment and Development: Agenda 21*, Geneva: UNESCO.

WCED (1987) *Our Common Future: The Brundtland Report*, Oxford: Oxford University Press.

References for Chapter 17

Burns, R.B. (1982) *Self-Concept Development and Education*, London: Holt, Reinhart and Winston.

Burns, S. and Lamont, G. (1995) *Values and Visions: Spiritual Development and Global Awareness in the Primary School*, London: Hodder and Stoughton.

Cox, E. and Cairns, J. (1989) *Reforming Religious Education*, London: Kogan Page in association with the Institute of Education, London.

Department for Education and Science (1988) *The Education Reform Act: Religious Education and Collective Worship*, London: HMSO.

Dewey, J. (1975) *Moral Principles in Education*, Harvard: Harvard University Press.

Diamond, C.T. Patrick (1991) *Teacher Education as Transformation: A Psychological Perspective*, Milton Keynes: Open University Press.

Fisher, S. and Hicks, D. (1985) *World Studies 8-13: A Teachers' Handbook*, Edinburgh: Oliver and Boyd.

Grimmett, M. (1987) *Religious Education and Human Development*, Great Wakering: McGrimmons.

Hammond, J. et al (1990) *New Methods in RE Teaching: An Experiential Approach*, Edinburgh: Oliver and Boyd.

Hay, D. (1987) *Exploring Inner Space*, London: Mowbrays.

Hicks, D. and Steiner, M. eds. (1989) *Making Global Connections: A World Studies Workbook*, Edinburgh: Oliver and Boyd.

Hirst, P. and Peters, R. (1970) *The Logic of Education*, London: Routledge Kegan Paul.

Hunt, D.E. (1991) *The Renewal of Personal Energy*, Toronto: The Ontario Institute for Studies in Education.

Jung, G. (1958) *Collected Works: Vol 1 X Parts 25ff and 23f*, London: Routledge Kegan Paul.

Kohlberg, L. (1980) 'Stages of Moral Development as a Basis for Moral Education', in Munsey, B. ed. *Moral Development, Moral Education and Kohlberg*, Birmingham Alabama: Religious Education Press.

Kragh, G. (1993) 'The Medicine Wheel: On Personal Development in the Teaching of Psychology' (unpublished paper presented at a meeting of the Erasmus Project, Education for Citizenship in the New Europe).

Mead, G.H. (1935) *Mind, Self and Society*, Chicago: University of Chicago Press.

OFSTED (Office for Standards in Education) (1994) *Spiritual, Moral, Social and Cultural Development: A Discussion Paper*, London: HMSO.

OFSTED (Office for Standards in Education) (1995) Report presented on the post graduate secondary course at the School of Education. Manchester Metropolitan University.

Piaget, J. (1932) *The Moral Judgement of the Child*, London: Routledge, Kegan, Paul.

Pike, G. and Selby, D. (1988) *Global Teacher, Global Learner*, London: Hodder and Stoughton.

Power, F.C. and Power, A.M.R. (1992) 'A Raft of Hope: Democratic education and the challenge of pluralism', *Journal of Moral Education* Vol 21, No. 3.1992, p.195.

Richardson, R. (1982) 'Culture and Justice: Key concepts in World Studies and Multicultural Education' in Hicks, D. and Towney, C. (eds) *Teaching World Studies*, London: Longman.

SCM (Schools Curriculum and Assessment Authority) (1994) *Model Syllabuses for Religious Education, Model 1: Living Faiths To-day*, York: SCM.

Steiner, M. (1994) *Learning From Experience: World Studies in the Primary Classroom*, Stoke-on-Trent: Trentham Books.

Voiels, V. (1994) 'The Use of Artefacts in Intercultural Education' (unpublished paper presented to the 20th annual conference of the British Educational Research Association).

Index